TAKING YOU TO PLACES YOU WOULD RATHER NOT GO

a journey with cancer

JOHN P. RYAN, SR.

TRUE NORTH PUBLISHING

Printed in USA.

ISBN: 978-0-578-84763-4 (paperback)
ISBN: 978-0-578-84764-1 (ebook)

Cover and book design by Asya Blue Design

This book is dedicated to Nancy.
John's wife and fellow traveler.
Our mother. She knew all this and more.

"I tell you most solemnly, when you were young you put on your own belt and walked where you liked; but when you grow old, you will stretch out your hands, and somebody else will put a belt around you and take you where you would rather not go."
—John 21:18

"Where there is great love there are always miracles. One might almost say that an apparition is human vision corrected by divine love. I do not see you as you really are, Joseph; I see you through my affection for you. The Miracles of the Church seem to me to rest not so much upon faces or voices or healing power coming suddenly near to us from afar, but upon our perceptions being made finer, so that for a moment our eyes can see and our ears hear what is there about us always."
—Willa Cather, <u>Death Comes for the Archbishop</u>

"We are not human beings having a spiritual experience; we are spiritual beings having a human experience."
—Pierre Teilhard De Chardin, <u>The Phenomenon of Man</u>

Red River Valley

From this valley they say you are going
We will miss your bright eyes and sweet smile
For they say you are taking the sunshine
That has brightened our path for a while

Come and sit by my side if you love me
Do not hasten to bid me adieu
But remember the Red River Valley
And the cowboy who loved you so true

Won't you think of the valley you're leaving?
Oh, how lonely, how sad it will be?
Oh, think of the fine heart you're breaking
And the grief you are causing to me

As you go to your home by the ocean
May you never forget those sweet hours
That we spent in the Red River Valley
And the love we exchanged amid the flowers

CONTENTS

ENDORSEMENTS

"How can I ever adequately thank you for your father's book – for its beauty, its courage, its candor, its brilliance, its faith, its love – and for entrusting such an extraordinary gift to me? I have spent all day reading it, and it has entered deeply into my heart and my soul."

—Dr. Renee C Fox, Annenberg Professor Emerita of the Social Sciences, University of Pennsylvania; author of numerous books in the sociology of medicine and bio-ethics

"A religious believer's journey with cancer to unwanted yet courageously experienced places. A memoir of care of the soul. An intimate story of one man's end of life where fear of pain, anxiety and death come to be replaced by a mysterious but grace-induced calm and readiness. A book of wisdom for the art of living and dying. The very stuff that caring of memories is made of. I shall not soon forget the man or the memoir."

—Arthur Kleinman, MD, Rabb Professor of Anthropology and Professor of Psychiatry and Global Health, Harvard University; author of "The Soul of Care" and other books

"I knew John Ryan growing up. His daughter is a very close friend. In his memoir, Mr. Ryan shows us the pain, the suffering, and, in an inspiring way, the hoping that encompasses his daily journey with cancer. We see him grappling with the raw reality of the loss of living and being. He makes abundantly evident that it is mastering his unwanted journey that brings the sacred, what he called 'the eternal now', into the act of dying. He both captures and surrounds himself in God's mysterious grace and carries that grace with him. This, in turn, shows him the way forward and shows us the way – the way of living in the sacred."

—Nan Dobson, BSN, RN, Hospice Nurse and Volunteer

"I am understanding on a deeper level my hesitation regarding reading, and even more so, endorsing this extremely poignant book. John Ryan's book is a call to face and travel beyond our deepest fears. The book chronicles the last 39 months in a life. It speaks to large fears, but, more importantly, it speaks to the longing and desire we have to know the spiritual world and to know others in our lives more deeply. John describes himself as an introvert, hesitant to reveal himself, thereby making the experience of knowing him even more profound. John tells the story of his illness. He writes with candor and grace. He takes us inside his world, inside his relationships, inside his journey to an unwanted place, but, in a mysterious way, his book does much more. It evokes, motivates, reinforces a profound sense of renewal and tenderness and hope toward life and others. To quote Henri Nouwen, 'I appreciate your life, I love you for being you and making my life richer for knowing you'."

—Eileen Pitone, Psychotherapist, Wyndmoor, PA

Taking You to Places You Would Rather Not Go: A Journey With Cancer by John P. Ryan left me breathless and, above all, inspired by his courage, love of family, his spirituality, and by his indomitable will to never give up. He surely fought the good fight. Along his journey, he grew as a person and as a Christian by winning an intimate relationship with God through his suffering, prayer, and intense inner life. His companions along his journey are some of our finest spiritual writers; Thomas Merton, Henri Nouwen, and John S. Dunne. He learned from them and from his own soul-work that the ultimate wisdom of life is to surrender to God's will, 'Not My Will but Thy Will Be Done'."

—Robert Waldron, author of "Walking with Thomas Merton"
and "Walking with Henri Nouwen" and other books

"Your father was a special person. The honest and forthright way in which he examined his own mortality, and the faith which it strengthened, is striking. I can't imagine what it is like to have awareness of impending death and write such a lucid and detailed account. Far from detached, your father articulated his feelings and emotions, and certainly his faith, while describing the reality of terminal illness almost like a journalist. The strength he took from it and the dialog he had with his own beliefs, is described with great clarity and conviction. He was a student to the very end. Really, our courageous teacher and our faithful guide offering us markers in this uncharted terrain. His hunger to learn and understand, his faith, in his last months says something about the tenacity of the human spirit. He lived a rich life and lived it in a way that was examined and reflective. All these things are immense blessings."

—Stephen Murray, Berlin, Germany, a friend and former colleague of John's oldest son. They worked together at the Wharton Center For Applied Research in Philadelphia. Stephen met by good luck, John and Nancy, at the airport when they were traveling to Florida in 1993.

"I had the good fortune to meet John Ryan once. He, his son, and I had dinner in San Francisco. That California trip in October 1992, I came to understand, helped him in coming to terms with his illness. That trip is described in this book, The author generously shares his final journey, his last 39 months, with intimacy and grace. It is a very personal story that is honest in both the physical and emotional detail of coming to grips with the end of one's life. As a caregiver to my father in his final years of life, I found the narrative both instructive and comforting. Although each person's journey is unique, this story helped me be a more knowledgeable and caring companion to my father and better able to understand his reflections, fears, and ultimate peace during his final passage."

—Karen Wall, Human Resources Executive, Retired, Wilmington, North Carolina

"This book reminded me of my own father's 'unwanted journey'. Like John Ryan, he too showed remarkable strength, courage, optimism, while facing fears, terror, even despair at times. Since my father was a quiet man, I found John's insights and thoughts, his everyday coping and healing suggestions described in the 'call outs', particularly helpful. Most importantly, this book reminded me again, in new ways, how 'faith' can help us transform a fear of dying into a peaceful readiness for what John called the transition to 'the higher plane'. Anyone who is facing death (or has a loved one facing death) will find this book inspirational, instructive, and, most of all, comforting in making that 'unwanted journey'."

—Ted R. Gambill, Retired AAA Business Executive, Athens, GA

"This is not really a book about how to die, but rather a book about how to live. This is a story of courage and toughness that, at the same time, is framed with tenderness and the fragility of humanity. The spiritual insights, the references to family, and the story of a precious and enduring marriage is richly described in this book and in John Ryan's journals. A book that calls us to remember what really matters in life so that when we do reach that point of transition into another life, we can do it with no regrets."

—*Bob Fisher, President of Belmont University and co-author of*
"Life is a Gift--Inspiration from the Soon Departed"

Taking You to Places You Would Rather Not Go is written with a rich and wonderful voice full of remarkable clarity. The journey of John Ryan captures an arc that we will all travel, yet provides a powerful insight into how each of us can be better spouses, children, siblings, grandchildren, colleagues, and providers to those that are making this passage. The vignettes from the hospital are a clear-eyed and timely perspective on what so many people have faced in the hospital during the COVID-19 Pandemic. A treasured gift and an empathic call to action. Wonderful insights for today and tomorrow!

—*Kirk A. Keegan, MD, MPH; Chief of Urology and Assistant Chief of Surgery,*
Nashville VA; Assistant Professor, Vanderbilt University Medical Center

"How many of us have lost a loved one not knowing what was inside their head or heart? Instead, we are left with an unanswered question or the lingering fear of taking this 'unwanted journey' ourselves one day. When I lost my mother, thankfully I discovered two decades of my mother's heartfelt notes tucked in her little 'God Boxes'. John Ryan, a husband, a father to four, and a grandfather, as he progressed through his own arduous journey with cancer, and very fortunately for us, shared his most intimate thoughts, a priceless treasure. *Taking You to Places You Would Rather Not Go* captures the profound courage and brilliance of a human being facing life's ultimate test. His frank and revealing insights offer every reader an understanding shoulder as well as a ladder to step up to our most challenging journey."

—*Mary Lou Quinlan, Author, "The God Box,*
Sharing My Mother's Gift of Love, Loss and Learning to Let Go"

"People have long wanted an explanation for why bad things happen to good people. The Bible's oldest manuscript, the book of Job, grapples with this issue and the discussion may never end. Common wisdom in our time says ill fortune falls randomly across all humanity. That may be true. But so is this: some people have the makeup and experiences to wrestle with the horrors that life does bring—ordained or random—and are able to seek meaning. John Ryan, to our benefit, was one of them. I urge those who read this book, whether you are a newly diagnosed patient with a severe illness, a family member of the patient, a loved one, or a close friend, to do so with a highlighter in hand. Mark the parts that speak to your heart, to your place in this emerging drama. Then go back and read them periodically, like a devotional. John was able to mark a path. It was not straight. Few ways through a serious illness rarely are. And it may not be exactly the right path for your situation. But I believe his book will point you in the right direction."

—Bruce White, a former journalist and consultant, now retired;
friend of the Ryan family; Tabernacle, New Jersey

"This book is a call 'to begin again'. In reading and re-reading my Dad's book, I remembered a moment that speaks for itself. It was a Saturday morning. I was visiting my parents. It was late 1994. My Dad was very sick, then. We were in the kitchen. We often talked sitting in their kitchen. He was writing his book. He said it was 'grandiose' and 'self-serving'. Said he was going to stop. I listened. Time moved forward, and we talked about other matters. Before I left, I noticed he threw away the hand-written pages. I saw them in the kitchen waste basket. I took them out before I left and just left them on the kitchen table. I did not leave a note. The next day, my Mother called me. She said he was writing again. An everyday moment remembered. A moment of grace experienced that day. He moved forward writing his important book. 'Always, we begin again'. He taught me that."

—Pat Ryan Dice, John's daughter, Fernandina Beach, FL

FOREWORD

This book describes the moving spiritual journey of a remarkable man, John Ryan, told in his own words. While there are many accounts of terminal illness, few have achieved the candor and depth of spiritual insight on display in this volume. With a razor-sharp honesty, John Ryan describes his ups and downs, his fluctuations between despair and hope, and his search for a spirituality that transcends death. While the book is deeply grounded in the best of the Catholic Christian tradition, it explores the meaning of the sacredness of life and the far reaches of grace through an eclectic range of novels, spiritual teachings, and rituals of care.

Because John Ryan was spiritually and personally resourceful, and because he was generous enough to record his journey, he provides life lessons for all of us. He shows us how to respond with both realism and hope to a terminal illness. The courage embodied in his mantra - *fear is useless* - runs through his narrative. He also provides a powerful lesson in how to continue to care for one's family through the dying process, recognizing that dying is never only about the terminally ill, but about all those who love him.

This is a book of great value to all who inhabit this mortal coil.

Larry R. Churchill, PhD
Stahlman Professor of Medical Ethics Emeritus
Vanderbilt University

INTRODUCTION

This is a story of two miracles. A book that is both a memoir and a practical guide for others facing a serious illness. The book was written by my father, John Ryan. It documents his 39-month journey with stomach cancer, from February 1992 thru March 1995. It is a record of his struggles, his coming to terms, his learnings, his hopes. His narrative text was largely unedited. This book, his original 26,585 words, was handwritten. Additionally, John (his parents, his sister, his brother, his friends, called him Jack) kept several journals. We include excerpts from his private journals and letters in the appendices. We also identify 30 "call outs." They are highlighted in bold. These "call outs" serve as a summary of healing practices and every day routines that John followed and found helpful.

This book is an invitation to the reader to stand and walk with him on what he called "this unwanted journey." It is invitation to literally see through another person's eyes. Importantly, to see what gives shape and meaning to a life.

Two miracles. John asked and prayed for a first miracle, an additional two years of life. Later, after the gift of these two years, he prayed for a second miracle. "Miracle" is a word he used many times in his private journals. There were 13 references to his praying for a second miracle in his last 45 journal entries. He prayed for the miracle of "more time" but never in a selfish way. Always, acknowledging mystery at work here, the unfathomable mystery of God's way. His book tells the story of these miracles and shows us how he used his time and what he learned.

He wanted this book to be a short book and wanted it helpful for others. His original outline had five organizing points:

1. *"Book should be relatively brief, max 120-130 pages".*

2. *"Should be open, authentic, honest, believable and lay bare the weakness and strengths of the human condition."*

3. *"Book should speak strictly from where I am, who I am, and in order for the reader to understand 'ME.' A great deal of insights and anecdotal material from my family, e.g., bonus time, Mom, prayer, survival, cowboy songs, Red River Valley".*

4. *"Keep prose simple. Avoid complexities, although I think it is vital to explore my own painful reflections using Theology, Philosophy, and Revelation."*

5. *"Faith and hope and dominance of 'the Living God,' undiluted – let it permeate every chapter. Let the struggles surface. No saccharine. No sweet acceptance."*

6. His original outline shows additional chapters, which he never wrote.

His book was completed a month or so before he died. I view this book as a complete book, not incomplete in any fundamental way, true to what he wanted to say. It is not fragments stitched together from his private journals. It is an original book, a book he worked on diligently in the last six months of his life. It is a coherent book and, as you will see, it is a courageous book shaped by deep honesty and a deep faith.

The History of this Book

I do not know the precise date when he started writing his book separate from his private journal writing. His journals are longer than this book. His private journal is 31,080 words, 91 entries, all handwritten. He kept it in an old, 6 inches by 9 inches, black leather, 3-ring binder.

One of these journal entries show us how he thought about this task and his great clarity about the importance of this task and about his being prepared, focused, resolute.

"I am almost ready to begin writing but I know in starting this project it will begin to absorb me and I want to be sure I am ready for it."

I do not know exactly what he meant in saying *"I want to be sure I am ready for it."*

I wish I could have another day with him and could ask him about that and so much more.

I do not know what his writing process was. I do not know where he wrote. Was it at my parent's kitchen table or in his black leather chair in his bedroom? I do not know what time of day he wrote: early mornings, late afternoons, in the evening?

Indeed, much is known and much is unknown here. Our "knowing and not knowing" and the glimpses he left for us are, in a larger sense, very similar to how a life unfolds and really is. There is much we do not see in a lived life, whether our own life or in another person's life.

In the end, I believe we can best think of his book as a kind of field guide and map needed for a journey where there are no maps.

In brief, it is a guide at many levels, but three stand out, are distinctive and relevant to all of us:

1. Everyday coping practices that work
2. His exploring openly and honestly the deepest, the most fundamental questions in his life, where and how he found meaning, what his own "credo" was
3. Glimpses of his faith, what I see as a kind of Christian and Zen-like spirituality with emphasis on "the eternal now."

John kept several kinds of notebooks and journals. See Appendix 3 for excerpts from his private journal.

He read extensively during his illness. He liked serious writing--theology and philosophy. In fact, early during his illness, he drove to and attended and was very moved by lectures given in the evening by Rev. Leo Van Everbrook from LaSalle University. These talks were on the Theology of Death and Resurrection. He tape-recorded those lectures.

He read carefully and took detailed notes on many writers and thinkers. Henri Nouwen, Teilhard de Chardin, Karl Rahner, Morton Kelsey, John Sanford, John Donne, and John Carmody, were favorites. In a light blue spiral bound notebook, he had 13 pages of detailed notes on the Gospel of Luke. He also had a separate blue notebook dedicated to Victor Frankel and to philosophers that influenced Frankel. His notes are methodical and detailed like a faithful Ph.D. student. These books, which we still have, are filled with yellow magic marker highlighting and notes in the margins of the books. He liked the physician Bernie Siegel a great deal. He listened to his audiotapes and read several of his books and he "acted" in his everyday life on Siegel's practical suggestions about coping and managing a serious illness and about inner healing. He read Willa Cather's novel, The Death of an Archbishop and called it "pure writing."

He also kept a "dream journal." He dutifully recorded his dreams for almost six months. He lamented and had regret that so many of his dreams were work related versus symbolic and transformative dreams.

He excerpted articles from the Philadelphia Inquirer about current events. Occasionally, he wrote a letter to the editor. He listened to talk radio. Loved music: classical, the big bands of his youth, and country music in his later years.

During the middle of his illness, during a year of remission, he wrote gratitude letters to his brother and sister and his four children. He did not write a letter to his wife. He reflected on that deliberate omission in his private journal. He said "she knew all this" and for Nancy "words were not needed." We include one of these gratitude letters, a letter to his daughter, his youngest child, in Appendix 4.

Also, see Appendix 5 for a letter he wrote to a Men's Faith Sharing Group. Here, we see John as a teacher. We see here his deep introspection, inner honesty, humility, and, importantly, his sharing his own lessons learned.

His writing was known to his family, but he was private about it. Stoical, in the best sense.

He gave all his journals to me, gave them without any fanfare, before he went into the hospital.

Fear is Useless.

The poignant opening pages of his book describe the deepest levels of human fear. We see a man in a hospital, in the intensive care unit, recovering from a six-hour surgery. He is awake at 2 AM and we see through his eyes.

We, his family, were thankful that he had survived the surgery. Yet that night we were overwhelmed, disoriented, lost in many ways, physically and emotionally exhausted.

Then and there, however, he was alone and he carried inside what he called "a brutal, punishing terror." A fear and a reality different from our experience.

More than two years later, as he described on the first page of his book, we get just a glimpse of this fear.

"Everything became crystal clear. Panic hit, and hit hard. The hopelessness of my situation. The death sentence of terminal cancer. The loss of my loved ones. The total disintegration of my life. All these thoughts flooded my consciousness with pristine, brutal clarity. The demons had come out in full force, malevolently, with no compassion and were relishing the kill. The panic and terror increased and I was pushed into this vortex of despair which could only end in my total destruction."

We travel with John through the ups and downs of facing the end of life. He describes clearly, almost clinically at times, what he saw and felt. He describes his largest fears, the darkness inside, the anxiety, sadness, depression that are a cancer patient's traveling companions. The other side of this fear is courage and moments of heartfelt joy and equanimity. We see John find his courage, his will, his resolve. We see him find meaning in his illness. We see his deepest character strengths unfold. Importantly, he describes his own inner transformation. He describes and explains the great gift of peace that he experienced so mysteriously one night in that ICU hospital unit. That peace was his first miracle. John prayed for his fear to pass. He prayed for a miracle, for more time, for that terror and fear to pass, and he tells us that he received the true gift of "peace." A "peace" that was given mysteriously, out of the blue, given by a Higher Power, given by a God he believed touched him.

This book describes his experience both in the early days and nights in that intensive care unit and in later months in learning to live beyond this fear.

He tells us very simply that "fear is useless." Trust is needed. A deep faith. A world view takes shape here, becomes his bedrock, as he becomes a new man, becomes his deeper self, his true self.

John was a thinker more than a feeler. As such, he questioned this fear and he questioned, and reality-tested (like a good scientist) the peace he was given. We see his doubts. We see his recurrent fears and anxieties over his 39-month journey with cancer. We see his persistence, that courage, that faith, he carried inside over this long journey. We see, from the inside, through his eyes, glimpses of what he experienced. We see his meaning making and we see his faith-driven worldview come alive. Simply put, we see this man made whole. Also, we see his gradual detachment from everyday life, his clear intent to pay attention and come to terms with the end of his life, and his slow and steady movement into what he called "the eternal now."

In many ways, the core motif and central message of this book is that "fear is useless." A message important for other fellow travelers facing a serious illness. In reading this book, we come to understand why. We see that fear is real but learn that "fear is useless" and we see how one man found his way beyond this fear and the demons of cancer.

The Gift of Time

John's first miracle was the gift of more time--two years of additional life. He received what he prayed for. He was deeply grateful for this additional time and he used it wisely. In a literal way, his second miracle was not granted, at least not in the way he hoped for. He was not granted additional time beyond those two years. He often prayed for more time to live and wrote about that in his journals. However, I believe he learned another kind of time. A time different from chronological time. He learned about symbolic time, a time of pure mystery and silence, a kind of transcendent time, what we might think of as timeless time. He called this "the eternal now." There are many references to this "eternal now," both in this book and in his private journals. He tried to the best of his ability to prepare for and be worthy of that time. In this way, I believe his second miracle was fully granted. He was given the gift of living in two dimensions.

John's book and his journals chronicle his journey in time. See Appendix 1 and 2 for a biographical profile and a detailed timeline of his illness.

We see him in the ICU ward. We see him at home with his wife navigating the ups and downs of this illness. We see him with his doctors and working through treatments. We see him taking trips to California, seeing Big Sur, and to the Jersey Shore, and Florida. We see many memorable visits with his children and we read about his conversations with them. We come to understand his hopes for his children and grandchildren. We see heartfelt visits with his brother and sister and we read about the gratitude letters he sent to them and his four children.

Also, we see visits from his good friends. We see glimpses of private moments. Dancing with his wife in their Weymouth Place kitchen with country music playing when they received news of his remission. We see private moments of anguish endured. We see a man fully aware. A man grateful for the additional time he was given, and yet fearful and in pain at times--but also filled with deep faith and often joy. We see a man whose life was well-lived. A man who left nothing unsaid. A man always there, always present, never absent, never not there, for his wife and their four children. We see a husband, a father, a brother, a son, a grandfather, a mentor, a teacher, a writer, maybe a saint.

The poet William Stafford writes that "the world happens twice; once what we see it is; second it legends itself deep, the way it is." John's book "legends itself" in us in that way. We come to know him in this book. He is our faithful guide and a grace-filled fellow traveler who shared what he discovered in his fateful journey with cancer.

CHAPTER I: SHOCK - THE EARLY DAYS

It's 2:00 in the morning. It's as quiet as the intensive care unit of a hospital gets. Sounds of shuffling feet, muted conversations and the purring, whirring, disconcerting sound of machines and sophisticated equipment going on and off– these all become part of your environment and let you know you are in a strange, surrealistic place you would rather not be. Time is a vague reality. You know that you spent a previous night in this strange new world, but days and nights seem to merge into shades of light and darkness with no sense of meaningful activity. Your mind is at work, teeming with contradictory thoughts. When it begins to focus too long on a single thought, the thought begins to break apart and dissipate into a vague, meaningless abstraction, with dark elements of terror lurking just beneath the surface. Your mind mercifully turns off before the demons are allowed to surface.

The night can be lonely and terror-filled in the intensive care unit – you exist in this bizarre world as a captive with your body immobilized in a maze of tubes, wires, and restraints. So long as your mind slips out of reality before thought becomes clear you are able to survive.

At 2:00 a.m. on this fateful day, my mind didn't turn off. Everything became crystal clear. Panic hit, and hit hard. The hopelessness of my situation. The death sentence of terminal cancer. The loss of my loved ones. The total disintegration of my life. All these thoughts flooded my consciousness with pristine, brutal clarity. The demons came out in full force, malevolently with no compassion and were relishing the kill. The panic and terror increased, and I was pushed into the vortex of despair, which could only end in my total destruction. A brutal, punishing terror overwhelmed me. It was choking the life out of me and I was falling helplessly in endless black space. I was turning and twisting in an agony of despair. There was no way out. I knew then I was helpless and totally out of control, but it was only then at the very bottom of the pit, I was given the grace and wisdom to surrender, to give it up.

I turned to the Lord, to the Jesus of Mercy and Compassion and said simply: "Lord, I cannot handle this. I need your help." This simple, spontaneous prayer was probably the first real prayer, straight from the heart, that I had offered since my surgery. Prayer had seemed superfluous in the misty, drugged world I inhabited. But the clarity of vision in the face of stark, unrelenting terror made prayer not only a meaningful reality, but a last desperate hope for survival.

A strange and startling reaction! Within minutes I felt my body relaxing and the terrible tension leaving me. My tortured mind was no longer pounding with fear-driven anxiety. I began to feel peaceful and light.

Over the next ten minutes that peaceful wave, that welcomed presence, completely enveloped me. With almost a child-like reassurance from a motherly caress, I turned my head on the pillow and immediately fell into a long, peaceful sleep.

There are very few experiences in life that are so profound and meaningful that they remain in your consciousness forever. Most such experiences are mystical by nature, bordering on the edge of the spiritual. The experience defies explanation and perplexes the rational mind. Only a leap of faith or an intuitive insight provides the answer. Without doubt or reservation, I was visited in that dark night by the presence of God. His Divine Son, the God of Mercy and Compassion, heard the cries of a desperate man and came to his rescue and brought him peace.

I have had many rough moments since that night, fighting a tenacious, unrelenting disease, but never has that awful panic returned. The peace I was given was a permanent gift that will never be taken away. The meaning of the beautiful gospel passage "My peace I leave with you, my peace I give to you … Let not your hearts be troubled, neither let them be afraid…" is now abundantly clear to me. God's "peace" is God's "presence" as he joins us in intimate union and dispels the clouds of fear. This intimate union provides the unlimited resources of our omnipotent creator, an overflowing of His grace, which will sustain us and carry us forward to meet all that lies ahead.

What had happened to me in the last few days? How much had changed in the body I had before, the body that had given me sixty-four years of faithful service? Had it been ravaged by the surgeon's scalpel beyond repair, or would it ever return to its efficient state of normalcy again? These are questions that wandered through my troubled mind, begging for answers. Those answers awaited my surgeon's visit, which I was anxiously awaiting.

The only thing I was sure of was that I had survived major surgery, "big time" as my surgeon called it. I was told that I had been subject to six hours of major probing, cutting, removing and repairing. Fortunately, unlike Humpty Dumpty, they were able to put me back together again. Going into the first operation of my life, I had felt like someone entering a great mystery, an alien world of technology and medical magic that intimidated me. I remember as I was being wheeled down the corridor to the operating room that I prayed with earnest conviction that God would take me home if survival meant a life of helplessness and misery. But deep in my heart I wanted desperately to survive.

Finally, a visit from my surgeon, Dr. Pellechia, Chair of Surgery at Holy Redeemer Hospital. I should not fault him since relaxed yet serious conversations with a wired-up patient three days out of surgery in the intensive care unit are not easy conversations. If I were to script a model surgeon for a Hollywood hospital drama, I could not go wrong with Dr. Pellechia.

A virile, middle-aged athletic type who gives the aura of robust health, he invariably has a pleasant smile. Dressed in the light green garb of the surgeon, he is the essence of what may be called cool, and his whole demeanor seems to make a definitive statement – cool, competent, caring and professional. I can attest to the accuracy of all four qualities.

Due to my partially drugged state, Dr. Pellechia did not give me much detailed information. He indicated the operation was very successful, and they had removed all of the cancer. He was very happy with the way my system tolerated the surgery and felt confident that I would make a strong and successful recovery. No question that even with his short visit and lack of details he succeeded in pumping up and brightening my spirits. I learned later through more frequent exposure that Dr. Pellechia always operated on the sunny side of the street and was a dedicated optimist by nature.

My temporary home in intensive care was never a stable one. While the pain and discomfort were quite tolerable due to the controlled injections of morphine and whatever other chemicals were dripping through the intravenous apparatus, I was never comfortable in this strange environment. There was a continual apprehension as to what would happen next. I must mention how impressed I was with the "self-administered" morphine pump system I was hooked up to as a supplement to the automatic IV system. If pain developed, all I had to do was press the button of a control device and pain-killers were promptly injected into the solution. Ingenious and remarkably effective and safe, since the number of injections and dosage was pre-set with a maximum cut-off. The other benefit was psychological, knowing that you, the helpless, dependent patient, could alleviate your own pain.

While I was in intensive care for only five days, it seemed much longer. Each day saw improvements in my comfort level as various tubes and monitoring devices were gradually removed. I began to appreciate the short but welcome visits of my family members, that vital support team who would sustain me through the difficult month that lay ahead. Strange thought: in the intensive care unit the social ambiance seemed to wear itself out rather quickly and I felt almost relieved to return to my solitude. The most interesting and upsetting of my experiences in intensive care came during my fourth night. People come and go in this unit in complete anonymity, wheeled in and wheeled out, in most cases like rigid cadavers. You never meet your neighbors since each is assigned to his quiet little cell and nobody is ambulatory. However, everyone shares one common characteristic – everyone is very, very sick.

The afternoon of my fourth day a patient was wheeled into intensive care and placed in a room two doors down from me. He must have had a large family since several groups of people came in to see him during the late afternoon and early evening hours.

I thought it unusual to have that many visitors admitted since the man was comatose and had, no doubt, just recovered from a major operation and was possibly in critical condition. But all was quiet and eventually the unit settled into the quieter, more muted feel and rhythm of the night.

Suddenly, just past midnight, a commotion occurred just outside my door, which was half ajar. I was resting, half asleep, and was immediately wide awake with the sound of many people literally running into the area. While sounds were somewhat muffled, there was the unmistakable intense dialogue of doctors and nurses working feverishly on my neighbor. This drama continued for almost a half hour. Then, all was quiet. I was straining to catch any conversation I could overhear, but one of the nurses had closed my door almost shut, which muffled sounds from outside my room. I desperately wanted to know what was going on since I felt a real affinity and empathy to the plight of this poor man.

Possibly another half hour later, I heard the sounds of people in the area, no doubt family members who had been notified. As they passed my door, I distinctly overheard a doctor make the statement that the patient had been stabilized and a massive heart attack occurred unexpectedly. He indicated they had done everything possible to save him but it was too late. Other family members came in later, stayed only briefly and left. It was only a short time later that the body of my neighbor, broken in a sudden violent paroxysm of death, was wheeled out of the area. Another chapter closed, another story ended. I prayed for my unknown and fellow sufferer.

Death is an anathema to modern society. Vast sums are spent to avoid it, forestall it, soften it and hopefully, in the most sanguine vision of enlightened science, to eliminate it. From birth on, we are shielded and desensitized to its existence, which works to a degree during the exuberant stages of youth, through the robust vitality of middle age, and even into the early glow of the golden years. But then the specter begins to resurrect. Buried too long and banished from the arena of life, it begins to appear, initially as a mild irritant, but gradually as a very uncomfortable anxiety just beneath the surface which refuses to be ignored any longer. Man is forced to face his mortality head on, totally unprepared by a life of denial. Many panic.

Those of us with a terminal illness face this ultimate reality prematurely and unexpectedly. Our mortality is essentially the same, but with a profound difference. The difference is time – an enigma to philosophers from the dawn of reason. This elusive measuring rod of life's processes, indeed of the entire cosmos, has suddenly wound down. It will shortly stand still and merge into the timeless reality of the Godhead from whence it came, the journey from Alpha to Omega in Teilhard de Chardin's language.

You may wonder at my lapse into heavy metaphysics and theology, but at some point, in this process everyone begins to philosophize and come to grips with ultimate ends and the real meaning of life.

There is no question that the sudden death of my hospital neighbor left me rattled. When you are living near the edge of the precipice, it doesn't take much to push you to the brink and to find your imagination running wild. I wrestled with the demon called fear that night and once again experienced the anguish of being helplessly imprisoned in this finite body, over which I no longer seemed to have any control. But strange to say, there was no sense of panic as on that night earlier in the week when panic reigned supreme and, miraculously, the Lord came to me and brought me His peace. The aura of His peace gradually set in and I was able to sleep, not exactly in a state of blissful tranquility, but certainly in a state of controlled anxiety.

One other vivid memory played out in my mind during the days in intensive care. It was a stark flashback of my first moments when my gastroenterologist announced that I had cancer. Thoughts of this kind can be so realistic that you virtually relive the experience in all its pathos, pain and terror. When Dr. Lescowitz had completed his endoscopic examination several weeks ago, I knew there was some sort of 'mass' lodged between my esophagus and stomach, which would require a biopsy to indicate whether it was malignant or benign. He wanted to see me in a week to review the results of the tests.

Several days later, my wife and I were returning in the evening from our restaurant, which we were operating at the time. I activated my answering machine to find a message from Dr. Lescowitz requesting that we reschedule my visit the following evening at 9:00 p.m. It didn't take a genius to discern some ominous conclusions from this troubling message. Busy doctors don't re-schedule visits on such short notice unless something urgent is involved, and last appointments are usually indicative of the need for undisturbed patient time. Add to this the known presence of a 'mass' on the esophagus and biopsy results probably now confirming a diagnosis. What do you get? Bingo! Malignant tumor! Cancer.

My wife Nancy and I didn't say much, although we were both, no doubt, experiencing the same thoughts and feeling the same intense emotions. Human nature is strange indeed. Even in the most intimate relationship we shy away from confrontation with reality that threatens us and renders us naked and vulnerable. We talked it out that evening, never once mentioning the word cancer, and talked ourselves into the feeling that it was something that could be taken care of and corrected. Privately, I was thinking the worst – inoperable cancer and a death sentence.

My son Michael drove us to Dr. Lescowitz's office. Nancy, no doubt, had the premonition that support might be needed that evening. Sure enough, we were the last patients of the evening and the nurse wasted no time in ushering us into a small, private office. We sat down and waited apprehensively with little to no conversation. Time and eternity approach each other in such circumstances and in total conflict – time demanding action and a quick verdict, and eternity holding back the floodgates to forestall the impending doom. The door of the office was partially ajar and I could see Dr. Lescowitz in the next room pacing back and forth with a troubled, anxious look on his face. Our eyes met briefly and almost immediately and resolutely he walked into the office. I felt sorry for him. He sat down at his desk and gave it to us straight. Bad news. The growth was well developed and cancerous. It would require an immediate operation.

There is no shock in the world quite like the pronouncement that you have cancer. It crashes into you with an emotional charge that obliterates any chance for rational judgments and reasoned response. I could feel the audible gasp from Nancy and the quiet tears followed. Michael, who by nature is the taciturn, self-contained cool type, said nothing, but the ashen countenance betrayed the shock that had hit him. See footnote 1 at the end of this chapter for more detailed information.

The urgency of the operation was apparent. Left alone the continued growth in this area would choke me to death. Dr. Lescowitz had acted fast, had been in consultation with our family doctor, Dr. Segal, and both had agreed that Dr. Pellechia was our best choice. He had already set up the appointment with Dr. Pellechia. Dr. Lescowitz had been thorough, compassionate and reassuring during our hour-long visit. Our traumatic visit gave me a new perspective on one of the doctor's roles in serious disease. He surely must die a little with each patient he must inform, and I suspect that no matter how often these melodramatic and agonizing scenes are played out in his office, the impact is no less difficult for him.

Today, good news. The doctor came in and removed the big draining tube inserted in my side—one of the areas that had been giving me the most trouble. Over the past two days, the tubes in my throat and nose had been removed, one by one, so other than the IV paraphernalia that was still hooked up, I was almost unwired, a comparatively free man.

Speaking as a novice in hospital culture, I should comment on the extraordinary phenomenon of the art of catheterization. Never having experienced it and unable to explore the multiple hook-ups to various body parts, (particularly orifices of any kind), I was concerned that I hadn't yet needed to urinate. I finally asked one of my nurses who explained how they had taken care of the problem and reassured me that I would be on my own the next day.

All in all, now that my short stay in the world of intensive care was coming to an end, I found myself reflecting on my experience in a positive way. The staff, both day and night, had been exceptionally nice. They evidenced a high degree of professional confidence and a compassionate, caring approach that was not feigned or acted out – it was real.

The gift of touch is an obvious blessing in some people. Their soft, caressing hands can move the wracked and mutilated body of a sick person and make him comfortable. Touch reached the level of an art form in some people. Back rubs and massages have a therapeutic effect much beyond the immediate physical sensation. Psychologically, it is the mother/child relationship of touch and healing that breaks through and warms the soul.

The intensive care experience was winding down. I had come from the netherworld of shadows and disorientation, and awakened into the conscious world of abject fear and panic. I had survived. That survival was conditioned heavily on my visit from God, that moment of grace when the Lord answered my pleas and gave me His peace. Quoting Psalm 34, "this poor man cried out to the Lord and He heard him and saved him of all his troubles."

The skeptics of the world will say my visit from God was nothing more than a self-induced psychological positive act of mind that gave me the relief I needed. I know deep in my heart the strength I received was far greater than anything that came from me. The peace it brought is a permanent gift that has withstood many trials that have come my way in the last two years. I am confident the gift of peace will continue to hold me up in the always-uncertain future. I can only say with faith and conviction, "praise the Lord, His peace be with you as it is with me."

Footnote

1. Below, we see "that drive" John wrote about but we see that moment through his youngest son Michael's eyes. For John and Nancy, they faced that night the hardest moment in a life. The reflection below by Michael was written more than 25 years after that fateful drive. It helps us see inside the silence he describes. A silence present as they faced the unknown. A silence where great fear is present and great courage born.

"Remembering That Drive"

I'm not quite sure why I was asked to make that drive that night to the Doctor's office. "They knew". Really, I believe we all knew. No words were needed. We feared the worst. As you can imagine, leaving their home around 8:30 PM that evening and driving to the Doctor's office and afterwards going back to my parent's home was hard. A night filled with deafening silence. The silence of shock. We were numb.

As I have thought about that evening over the years, I believe I was chosen for that drive because I am a man of few words and subdued emotions and that was what they most needed. They needed someone who would be unflappable. The feelings and the reactions we had that evening were largely unspoken but they were well understood by all and my parents knew I would be strong for them.

What did I see?

I saw my Mom almost immediately assume the role of the "right-hand man" in defiance of the fear that I knew consumed her.

I saw my Dad take a heavyweight punch like I had never seen anyone do before. I saw his incredible strength, his courage, his bravery. I had always thought of my Dad as being a very strong man, but this was different. Being there, being present with him, showed me that he was even stronger, a better man, than I had ever imagined.

That drive that night was a great gift. Being present with them in that difficult time is something I will never forget. My parents were loving and generous. They gave much to me during our time together on this earth but making "that drive" with them that night was perhaps the greatest gift of all.

CHAPTER II: A TEST OF FAITH – DAMAGE CONTROL

A big day. I am finally released from intensive care and assigned to a new home. My feelings are decidedly mixed in the sense that I am quite happy to leave a place of isolation which you share with a world of machines and technology, and yet you sense you are leaving a haven, a security blanket of sorts where sudden changes in your condition can be handled efficiently.

The nurses who had been with me during the past five days were gracious and caring and I wished I could take them with me to my new home. But I knew they were a special breed, trained for the demanding job of caring for the acutely ill person, whose fate frequently hangs by a thread, and where errors or slips by the nursing staff could have critical consequences. I marveled at their ability to leave their tour of duty each day, return to their mundane jobs of raising a family and taking care of a house, and return the next day to the tensions of the intensive care unit. I wondered what the burn-out rate must be.

My new room was a delightful change of scenery. Located in a comparatively new wing of the building, the décor consisted of soft and gentle pastels with attractive, functional furniture. What elevated my spirits most though was a large window joining me once again with the world of nature. It was a revelation to see the world outside again, in spite of the fact that it was a dreary February day with that typical leaden sky that goes with February. I hate February, even though the most momentous events of my life occurred in February; my marriage and the birth of my first child. I have added my first confrontation with mortality and my operation. Quite a month, February.

I was now situated comfortably in bed, assisted by two extremely competent nurses, with minimum hook-up now to an intravenous system. All other tubes and apparatus were gone. Today was a special day for another reason; I was to begin eating regular food again, even though the soft diet prescribed was to prove bland and tasteless. But here I was, clean and comfortable, in a pleasant room with only minor pain which I could control. The world seemed much brighter with the change in location.

In the early afternoon, my wife and other members of the family began filtering in and I soon had a roomful, literally, of love and support. What a change to be able to have everyone with you in a pleasant atmosphere where people felt free to laugh and talk normally again. Quite a contrast to the restrained, unnatural short visits in intensive care. I thoroughly enjoyed the love and friendship of my family and never appreciated more what a great gift they were in making my life meaningful.

The nurses began bringing in cards and flowers that had accumulated for several days and soon the room was filled with these beautiful tokens of love and friendship. Even the ubiquitous get-well balloons, with their happy faces and brilliant colors stood tall and cheerful in the room. Actually, I like them. They are a wonderful counterpoint to the solemnity and formal beauty of flowers, a playful infusion of levity to a serious scene.

Again, in the evening we had the parade of visitors and a repetition of the chitter-chatter and small talk I enjoyed so much in the afternoon. Eventually though, you begin to peter out and look forward to the solitude and quiet of being alone. By 9:00 p.m., everyone had gone and I was able to lie back peacefully and reflect on a most momentous day. The nurse made me comfortable with a nice soothing back rub, gave me my medications for the evening, and I was all set, hopefully, for a peaceful night in my new environment.

This was not to be. Although I was quite comfortable and had listened to some soothing music and felt pretty much at peace, my mind gradually slipped into a melancholy side of my nature. Then, the specific fears, which had no doubt been buried temporarily in my sub-conscious mind, began to surface.

Questions began to spill forth; were they conning me, giving me only the bright side? Did they really remove all of the cancer or was there a hidden residue waiting to erupt and spread like crabgrass? Would I be so ravaged by the extensive surgery that I could become a virtual invalid, incapable of doing the things that made life meaningful? The questions kept brewing up all infused with variants of morbidity and mortality. The cumulative effect was to sink me into a pit – a pit of hopelessness and self-pity, a deadening experience.

Finally, I tried to shut down my mind, to turn off this wonderful gift of consciousness, which is our greatest blessing as human beings and makes us most like God and yet, paradoxically, can be our greatest curse. We would pay dearly for the ability to turn it off at will and get respite from its relentless presence. I believe that is impossible, no matter how adept we may become at mind control or autohypnosis.

I do believe that we can transcend our consciousness, which is totally related to time and space, and move into a higher dimension related to eternity and spiritual reality. This transition from the here and now to the limitless reality of the eternal now can be attained, and only to a limited degree, through prayer and meditation.

I prayed and prayed, with as much fervor as I could muster, that God would take care of me, that with childlike simplicity, I might ask that He make me better.

Funny how when your own resources are exhausted and you realize how totally dependent you are, you become childlike and you turn with childlike faith to the one who can save you.

I gradually calmed the anxieties that had gripped me and felt my sense of peace restored. Thanks to God that at no time did that total sense of panic emerge. The demons did not return that night. I believe they had been effectively exorcised by the gift of God's peace, which I received several nights ago. I hope to God they never return.

The following day was a good day. I felt relaxed and comfortable with no significant pain. When the onset of pain became apparent, I again had access to that marvelous little device, the automatic pump, which injected the right amount of morphine into the system to control the pain. I had been sitting in a chair for short periods of time, but today I became ambulatory; I took my first walk. Of course, I was assisted by a nurse and had to haul my IV apparatus along with me, but the exhilaration of walking again was just a great experience.

Welcome visits from the family and a few close friends contributed greatly to an uplifting of my spirits. The telephone brought me back the real world with pleasant conversation with friends and associates, and in the center of all this activity you can very quickly begin to feel normal again. The stark realities of your condition begin to fade away amidst the social activities. This somewhat euphoric turn of events did not last. The next day or two shattered this illusion with the visit of the three wise men—my euphemism for the major doctors who were taking care of me.

My first visitor was Dr. Pellechia, my surgeon, who popped in bright and early in the morning, exuding his usual charm and vivacity. He sat on the edge of my bed and we chatted amiably for several minutes. He then brought me up to date on what he had done and where I was, medically speaking, and to a degree, where I was heading.

The surgery had been extensive, more than they had anticipated. They had cut through the chest and stomach area and located a large tumor in the upper part of the stomach, spreading into the esophagus to a considerable depth. They removed as much of the tumor as possible through the first incision, but found it impossible to reach the entire mass. The decision was made to cut through the back, with an incision stretching from the upper right shoulder blade down to the waist. Apparently, by opening up the whole back with the long incision, they were able to clamp open the ribs and reach the vital organs. They successfully removed most of the remainder of the mass, but found that the tumor lodged directly across the aorta of the heart.

The doctor indicated that he was ready to go into the aorta itself, but, fortunately, found that the growth had not penetrated into the aorta. They removed fifteen lymph nodes, of which twelve were malignant.

The final tally or damage assessment: over one half of my stomach had been removed, three quarters of my esophagus, and fifteen lymph nodes. The liver and lungs seemed to be healthy. Since the tumor had breached the wall of the stomach and the esophagus, there was a good chance that the cancer could spread through the blood stream. The lower part of my stomach had been stretched up to the small remaining portion of the esophagus and sutured at that point, leaving me a stomach capacity that resembled a narrow tube or flask, hardly the digestive capacity for a robust appetite.

At this point, I was in a state of shock over the extensive nature of the surgery and the radical extent of the disease. This tumor had been developing, unnoticed, for two to three years without symptoms and is rightfully designated as one of the "silent killers." Another month or two without surgery and I would not have survived.

A man would be living in a fool's paradise not to know the impact of this conversation. It was "Grimsville," pure and simple. You were on a short life line and your mortality was staring you in the face. Any other prognosis would be pure self-delusion and a flight from reality. In spite of positive assurances from my ever-optimistic surgeon that much could be done through radiation and possibly chemotherapy, I could see my prognosis in no other way except short-term, six months at most. Funny, no one would come out and say this; perhaps the obvious need not be said.

I am sure my family picked up immediately on my dramatic change of mood when they came to visit me that afternoon. Even though they had been more knowledgeable about my condition than I had been, they were still disturbed and apprehensive as I discussed in detail my morning consultation with my surgeon. We were not an upbeat group that afternoon and each of us had difficulty putting a positive spin on the facts that had been divulged. Somehow or other we talked our way through the grim scenario and, strangely enough, ended on a note of hope and optimism.

Of one thing I am sure in confronting serious illness – do not allow yourself to bury your fears and anxieties deep within. Share them with the people who love you, and without question, all who are involved in this human drama will emerge stronger, and with a deeper bond of compassion and a renewed sense of hope.

The second of the three wise men visited me on the following morning. He was identified to me as a radiation oncologist whom I had not met previously and who had been requested by my surgeon and family doctor to review my case and make his recommendations. A nice young doctor, professional in approach and apparently knowledgeable in his specialty. As it turned out later he would not handle my radiation therapy, but this has no bearing on the present situation. He indicated a radiation program of thirty treatments should be implemented, focusing solely on the original site of the cancer – the stomach and esophagus area. With radiation he indicated a recurrence possibility of twenty five percent or less. It seemed to be a clear-cut decision to go with radiation since both the surgeon and my family doctor concurred in his opinion. At the conclusion of this very brief but effective meeting, I indicated I would make a decision shortly.

And finally, the troika was completed the next evening with the appearance of Michael Spiritos, the last of the three wise men. And what a visit it was. My wife and daughter were in the room when Dr. Spiritos made his appearance. Since none of us had met him, he introduced himself as a medical oncologist who had reviewed my case on the advice of Dr. Segal, my family doctor. Perhaps sensing my nature, which is to know the facts, unvarnished and straight up, he proceeded to lay it on the line in technical, unemotional terms. No small talk, a straight, no-nonsense clinical exercise.

My wife and daughter were visibly shocked by the bluntness and directness of Dr. Spiritos' approach. Since he undoubtedly felt it was more efficacious to by-pass the sensitivities and communicate the facts, perhaps even he was not fully aware of the devastating effect his approach had on his audience. I don't know whether the medical schools spend a great deal of time and training on the human side of patient care, not to mention the holistic approach advocated by so many today, but my young oncology specialist was clearly on the side of blunt disclosure of the facts.

What he said was disconcerting and shattering to our hopes that evening. In his opinion chemotherapy was probably useless in my case. No medical protocol had yet been developed for stomach cancer that has proven more effective than doing nothing. He indicated that my cancer had been very extensive and well developed, had broken through the stomach and esophagus walls, with extensive lymph node penetration, and probably entered the blood stream. Injecting chemicals into the bloodstream with such possible broad disburse-ments was like "shooting a gun in the forest" the target was undeniable and elusive. Under these circumstances, chemotherapy would accomplish little or nothing to forestall the spread of the disease from its original site (metastasis of cancer cells), and only subject me to an unpleasant and troublesome period from side effects. Recommendations – no chemotherapy. End of story.

While all of us were upset by the apparent closing of one widely used therapy to cure cancer, we continued to question Dr. Spiritos on the nature of chemi-cal intervention and his experience with cases of my type. What disturbed us most, I believe, was the probable widespread dispersion of malignant cancer cells throughout the whole system, which Dr. Spiritos had depicted as almost a certainty. We were all neophytes in cancer pathology, and the prospect of numerous cancer cells marauding unimpeded in the body indicated an almost hopeless, morbid conclusion. While he emphasized the importance of my immune system in fighting off this invasion, it did not dispel an aura of hopelessness that he had created. I think he became acutely aware of this, among other things, and suggested we might want to obtain a second opinion.

Needless to say, my wife and daughter left that evening feeling much lower in spirits than when they came in, and my own psyche was not exactly brimming over with confidence and enthusiasm. It looked like a long, painful night ahead.

One may question the wisdom of having the doctors let it all hang out and confronting the patient and his family directly with the facts, as brutal as they may be, but it does have the result of dispelling all the illusions and making everyone face the tough decisions.

Quite to my surprise, Dr. Spiritos popped into my room bright and early the next morning. Apparently, my wife had had a conversation with our family doctor concerning how disturbed she was over the blunt approach Dr. Spiritos used.

The dynamic of family-doctor-patient relationships is a complex one at best and the essential aspects of timing, communications and common understanding are so often misunderstood, particularly in complex medical situations where so many specialists are involved. I understand that in some specialized cancer centers the whole cancer team works as an integrated unit and communicates with patients and family in conference meetings both to review and confirm the diagnosis and to agree on a unified approach to treatment. This seems to be a very practical solution to the problem, but it is highly unlikely that the extensive network of hospitals and medical centers can ever be reduced to such specialized operations.

Dr. Spiritos proved to be a personable, compassionate doctor on this visit. He covered in great detail the extent and nature of my disease and the possible paths of development it might take. Talking it out, one-on-one in a relaxed manner took the edge off the problem and somehow diminished the tragic overtones and the pathos that these discussions had generated the prior evening. The conclusion reached was that I should obtain a second opinion from a reliable oncologist and he would be happy to meet with me and my family to review the options and plan further treatment.

We concluded our meeting on a note of mutual trust and respect which left me with a positive feeling of confidence in the integrity of this young doctor, a confidence that would prove to be confirmed in a rewarding and close relationship over the next several years.

Hospital life develops a routine of its own, quite different from what you are accustomed to. The tempo is dictated by medication schedules, monitoring of vital signs, bathing, washing, back rubs, meal times, assisted walking, testing, consultations, visitors, and rest. Surprisingly, rest, at least during the day, assumes a low priority, which you gradually begin to regret. The sheer volume of activities diverts the mind from undue pre-occupation with your problems, but at the same time something inside you wants "think time" to sort things out and begin to chart a course for the future.

Then, comes night and the atmosphere changes completely. The last of our evening visitors have gone, the nurses have freshened you up, made you comfortable and given you your medications. Then, it becomes ominously silent and you prepare yourself from your consciousness and the teeming mind begins to bring to the surface the important thoughts, the things that matter. There is no way of avoiding this confrontation. Your reflective mind in all its vaunted power begins to function in high gear and simply will not be denied. You had better then develop your own coping mechanism or you are in deep trouble.

I don't regard myself as a super religious person, although I can never recall a time in my life that I did not believe in the fundamental principles that have shaped my life. These principles can be very succinctly stated:

- The universe and all life is good.

- A benign and omnipotent God created the universe.

- The God I believe in is a personal, living God, rather than a force or energy or a nebulous higher power.

- I am important in God's eyes. I am a child of God.

- Jesus Christ is the Son of God and my mentor and guide and personal savior.

- We are destined for higher life and immortal life in union with God.

It is not my intention to engage in a theological treatise, but there are times in your life when you must drop all illusions of reality and confront the ultimate questions, those that shape your life and give it meaning.

If the meaning of your life is centered solely on the temporal, the here and now, then you may face some truly difficult times ahead as you try to live with your illness. Your coping mechanism is extremely limited since your whole world is tied up in temporary things that disappear with time. The bedrock of my faith is based solidly on permanent realities, which last forever. Strangely enough, we run our busy lives almost unconscious of the principles that make us what we are. Then comes a calamity, a life crisis that makes us sit up and take notice and we begin to clarify and define our beliefs. Perhaps this is a good example of the good that comes out of adversity.

During my ten-day stay in the hospital, I underwent so many changes in mood that at times I felt as though I was on an emotional roller coaster in perpetual motion with no fixed destination. My support systems and coping mechanisms were gradually being defined and, surprisingly, once set in place they have changed very little since. First and foremost is the total involvement of my family. What a bedrock of stability and reassurance comes from the loving care one receives from his loved ones. Nancy, my wife of forty-four years, is a beacon of light and a loving presence in my new, more dependent life. Her care and concern never cease, and I marvel at her strength, which I never suspected was there. Perhaps it is another example of that "Amazing Grace," that powerful medicine of the spirit, which surpasses all understanding.

My three sons and wonderful daughter were there at all times to support my wife in her hour of need and to give me an outpouring of love and concern that warms the heart and builds the spirit like no other force on earth. Most of us by nature are egoists, self-sufficient and seemingly in control of our lives. When all that changes, suddenly and dramatically, you are now almost completely dependent on others and it is a bitter pill to swallow.

Based upon my experience, the sooner you can let go of ego and accept your new dependent status, the better off your loved ones will be. It is an irony of human nature that we tend to erect a barrier between ourselves and the great outpouring of love that families bring to us in times of need. Don't fight the gift of love. It comes from God, who is its source. Accept it lovingly; revel in it and thank God for the great gift you have received.

Blessing can come from the most unexpected sources. My son Jack was a casual friend of Yvonne Kaye, an addictions consultant for many years, who has a late Saturday evening talk show program on WWDB radio. I had met Yvonne several times at our restaurant. She is a charming woman, a Brit, who can relate some gripping experiences of her days in war torn London when the rockets were droning in every night.

When you wake up in the morning and find your next-door neighbor's house obliterated by a direct hit, your perspective on life can be influenced quite dramatically.

However, Yvonne was a student of Victor Frankel, the famous Austrian psychiatrist who had survived four Nazi concentration camps and went on to develop and complete his optimistic system of "Life with Meaning" and inspire millions of people world-wide with his philosophy of hope and the power of the human spirit. During my illness, I have become familiar with Victor Frankel's work and have found it to be a fascinating approach to a philosophy of life, quite compatible with my Christian faith, even though it is what might be loosely described as a secular religious approach.

You can imagine my surprise when I answered the phone one morning and the unmistakable voice of Yvonne Kaye came through. She was most gracious and consoling and I could sense immediately her genuine feeling and complete empathy which is a hallmark of Yvonne's personality. It is a gift which only a few people have been blessed with, and one which Yvonne has put to good use in helping thousands of people through life's tough spots over many years, all too often with little or no personal return.

Yvonne promised to send me a book which she felt would be most helpful to me. It is Bernie Siegel's book, "Love, Medicine and Miracles," which has opened up a whole vista of hope and optimism for me.

To the cancer patient, I could not recommend any written source for guidance and inspiration more strongly than Bernie Siegel's work. He is a practicing surgeon with extensive medical background, but with a surprisingly rich storehouse of religious and psychological insights. Add to this a deep-seated warmth and sense of shared humanity, all wrapped up in a

beautiful holistic approach to medicine and life, and suddenly in your hour of need you have acquired a friend and confidant, a reliable partner on your difficult journey ahead.

I don't want to belabor the point, but I feel so strongly about the benefits of Bernie Siegel's work for cancer patients that I must re-emphasize its impact on my life at this critical time. I read and reread his books over the months ahead and listened on a daily basis to his tapes on meditation and therapy. I can say with conviction that following my faith and prayer life and the great support of family, that Bernie Siegel's influence was the most profound and efficacious in my battle to cope with the fear and debilitating trauma of advanced cancer. God works in mysterious ways, since it is through the medium of a casual acquaintance, that this great source of hope and consolation came my way. I shall always be grateful for the kindness and compassion of Yvonne Kaye.

My last days in the hospital were uneventful – routine visits from the doctors who added nothing new and who all agreed that I needed three or four weeks of recuperation at home before embarking on any programs of therapy. The extensive surgery had exerted its toll on my system. My weight was down by twenty pounds and my energy level at a low point in my life, a natural malaise that occurs when you are savaged by major surgery. However, I must say with some degree of amazement, I was remarkably free from pain, and since the removal of the network of stitches, my incisions were healing beautifully. My hat is off to Dr. Pellechia for a masterful "plumbing job," his euphemism for the complex and skillful work in which he is engaged. So, I close the chapter on my hospital experience, and with a sense of relief, made the journey home to lick my wounds and plan the next stage of this unwanted journey.

CHAPTER III: HOME SWEET HOME

There is an old George M. Cohen song of World War I vintage entitled, "Only 45 Minutes from Broadway, But Oh What a Difference It Makes." The trip from Holy Redeemer Hospital to our home is about 45 minutes and I can attest to the truth that "Oh What a Difference It Makes." The thought of coming home brought on a deep emotional feeling of just what it meant to "come home." Without indulging in over-sentimentalism, which this thought can certainly engender, one must conclude that in times of great stress, home represents the safe haven for both mind and body.

A complete change of mood seemed to overtake me with the return home. Here was familiar terrain where I felt realized and comfortable, you might say even relieved. Relieved? Yes, if one had seriously considered the possibility of not surviving the operation and not seeing home again.

When I arrived home, I realized just how tired and weak I was. My wife observed this and promptly ushered me upstairs to our bedroom. Normally this room is a most pleasant room, bright and sunny, but as luck would have it today had to be the exception. The room was dark and dreary, reflecting the typical leaden skies of February, a most depressing month.

It didn't take long to get comfortable in a nice, warm bed. Since I was beginning to feel more pain than usual, I took my allowable dose of morphine and before I realized it, I drifted off to sleep. I woke startled, having no idea where I was in time or space, still lost in some frightening dream world.

This ongoing symphony resonated in my brain and I was caught up in its turbulent and troubling theme – more reminiscent of Wagner or Mahler, than a soft pastoral theme of a Beethoven or Debussy. It was playing to the human drama, reaching down into the lower depths of pain and suffering. I knew these feelings were the forerunners of fear and panic, which can quickly overwhelm you and bury you in self-pity and hopelessness. What to do? I knew I had to get hold of myself and change the momentum. I had to divert my thought and feelings to higher good before I would sink in a quagmire. After all, I was home and getting back to normal. I was going to be all right and it would be only a matter of time until my life would be back together again.

Human consciousness is tough to control and discipline. It just doesn't respond peacefully to the prompting of your higher powers of reasoning. But again, as had happened so often during the past ten days, I reached out for help and prayed. To the believer this would make sense. To the unbeliever it would be nothing more than a foolish illusion, a superstition, a dying remnant of the Middle Ages. Prayer is not a magic bullet, a quick cure, but slowly and sometimes painfully it can restore peace. Faith and hope are revived and you are absorbed by the higher reality, which transcends time and space and admits of no limitations.

The first week home was a week of accommodation, getting used to a markedly changed body with its severe limitations on formerly much enjoyed eating patterns. I ate six mini-meals a day instead of my traditional breakfast, lunch, and dinner. This regimen may furnish the necessary nutrition, but it plays havoc with the aesthetics and sheer joy of good food. I realized later on how premature and unwarranted were my criticisms of this diet where the food at least tasted good and was enjoyable compared to my experience several months later when the ravages of chemotherapy and radiation literally destroyed the taste buds, produced nausea and stomach cramps, and reduced eating to a painful chore.

Decision time was approaching again, not the usual kind, which can be troubling enough, but these were of the "life and death" variety. It makes a difference. Here and now, the uncertainties can be mind-boggling. The number one decision was easy, a second opinion. Through the good offices of our family doctor, we shortly made arrangements for a second opinion from the cancer group at the University of Pennsylvania Hospital. An easy choice and a good one since this facility was well regarded as one of the premiere cancer centers in the country. A week later, this consultation was concluded and confirmed the original diagnosis and recommended therapy—radiation and possible adjutant chemotherapy to supplement the radiation.

There is a big grey area with regard to certain types of cancer and the effectiveness of the chemical approach. The more common types of cancers—breast, lung, leukemia--have well developed and documented protocols of chemotherapy and their relative efficacy. Stomach cancer is less common and the incidence of this cancer has been on a downward trend. There is no known, proven protocol for stomach cancer. However, the University of Pennsylvania Hospital has been participating in an experimental program that they felt had some limited success. Ultimately, after much soul-searching we opted for this approach on the theory that the potential side effects might be worth enduring since there didn't seem to be any other viable options.

You become familiar with the cancer game rather quickly if you want to become a survivor. In years past, it was rather common practice to keep the disease hidden from the patient, sort of locked in a vault with only the medical people and selected family members having access to it. Today, it has proven much more effective for everyone concerned to be totally involved and know the facts, particularly the patient. True, the verdict of cancer is still equated with a death sentence and consequently can create a profound feeling of hopelessness in the patient, which culminates in a serious erosion of the will to live. The other side of the coin can be much

more positive and beneficial. Knowing the prognosis and the facts, the patient can overcome his initial shock and deal with the problem, opting to look on the positive side rather than succumb to the ravages of self-pity and helplessness. When one looks into the matter objectively, there comes the realization that cancer does have survivors, at all states and at all levels. As Bernie Siegel points out in his book, "Don't condemn yourself with statistics. Everyone is unique."

There is another therapeutic benefit from choosing the positive approach. There is much evidence today both from legitimate, scientific studies and from anecdotal experiences recounted from many sources that mind/body relationships are critical to the human being and exert a profound effect in wellness/sickness. It is now generally considered by even the most mechanistic, reductionist members of the medical and scientific community that the mind has a profound impact on the immunological system. The immune system is the essential protection system of the body for fighting off disease of all kinds and protecting the body from all types of predators, including the nefarious errant cancerous cells gone amuck. Thus, it makes sense to me to see a strong correlation between a knowledgeable cancer victim fighting his adversary, utilizing all the powers of his immune system in collaboration with the best medical assistance he can find, translating the "will to live" into positive, beneficial results in the body.

Finally, after going through all the agonies of decision making, Dr. Segal, our family physician, who was the invaluable "generalist" in our project, laid it on the line with me. He reviewed the options clearly and succinctly and put it right on the line with me. The final, ultimate decision is mine. It's always that way in life. There always comes a point where you and you alone, with the vaunted gift of freedom must take personal responsibility and decide. I would be remiss if I didn't acknowledge an improved element in my decision-making. Throughout this whole nerve-wracking drama of decision-making, I had continuing consultations with my "Mentor and My Guide" asking the good

Lord that he might guide me to the right path. I know full well that a good father would never direct a son otherwise. The imagery of the "snake and the scorpion" came into mind.

Everything is settled. When my month of recuperation from surgery is completed, I will begin a long program of radiation and chemotherapy that will occupy a major portion of my life's activities over the next nine months. Dr. Richter, Chief Radiologist at Abington Hospital, will handle radiation and work in conjunction with Dr. Michael Spiritos who will be my oncologist. This will prove to be a very workable team whom I continue to have total confidence in. They share a nice blend of human concern and medical competence that makes a difficult life situation much more bearable.

The human mind works in devious ways. We seem to have a built-in controller mechanism that sorts out what is to be admitted to our consciousness and what is to be ignored. I believe the term "selective perception" is appropriate here. In the case of serious illness, the disease moves to front and center and begins to dominate our waking consciousness. All kinds of information from all kinds of sources are eagerly invited into our cerebral inner sanctum for minute analysis and dissection. This same stream of knowledge would have previously been ignored. This is just another marvelous aspect of the human mind, the ability to absorb knowledge, reflect upon it and make logical decisions. To know is one thing. To know that we know, moves us into a higher stratosphere.

My religious and spiritual life is the bedrock upon which my coping mechanisms are built. Where life has ultimate meaning and can be maintained with such a focus, then I can begin to place things in context, even the so-called catastrophic parts of life, such as a terminal illness. While I do not know why all the things that happen in my life happen that way, I sense intuitively that nothing is accidental, that all things have purpose, are part of the divine plan, and the plan is good. This mindset is the essential road to positive

thinking, the only road to the healing and restorative powers of the human person.

I'm sure there are many things available if one can find them, although more of the material I've seen tends to treat only one aspect of the problem. The best and most comprehensive books and tapes I've had access to are Bernie Siegel's. His medical knowledge and experience as a surgeon and intimate knowledge of the disease is supplemented by a profound insight into the psychological and spiritual needs of his patients. Another excellent source of guidance and encouragement came from reading several books by Larry Dossey, notably "Space Time and Medicine" and "Meaning and Medicine," works prepared by a physician with extensive practical scientific knowledge combined with a very humanistic and spiritually oriented outlook on life. I do not think it is accidental that the spiritual element plays a central role in making these books an authentic and meaningful source of encouragement to those of us suffering our way through our illness.

There are several authors in the spiritual realm I would strongly recommend. They have been extremely helpful to me in sorting out the conflicting current and turbulence of my life's troubled waters. Henri JM Nouwen, Morton Kelsey, John Sanford, Victor Frankl, Thomas Merton, C.S. Lewis, John S. Dunne, are some of the more helpful authors I have read. For the benefit of any interested reader who may want to explore some of these writers I will include a list of these readings at the end of the book. I am not as disciplined as a writer, nor in fact that pretentious, that I will prepare a bibliography for the various quotes and references I use. They are, for the most part, bits and pieces I quote and in line with my own interpretations of the material. Note: John never prepared this bibliography.

The dynamics of family life come forcefully into play at a time of profound crisis and shock. In my case, I see a close knit family unit – father, mother, three grown sons and one daughter – after forty years of stable, enjoyable, taken-for-granted family life suddenly turned upside down with a traumatic shocker – dad has cancer. I cannot enter fully into the individual minds of my family under normal circumstances, but when stark confrontation with death is thrust upon them, then the possibility of truly knowing what is going on inside becomes much more complex.

We all wear several faces, the persona we present to the world, our public face, which tells the world what we want them to see in us. And the private face, which we alone know. Unfortunately, the private face does not tell the whole story. The composite face we construct for ourselves, an amalgamation of good points and bad points, is designed to allow us to live with ourselves on a practical level and to feel reasonably good about ourselves. Unfortunately, we all tend to repress aspects of our nature which we avoid facing up to, the so-called "shadow side" of our personality in Jungian psychology. I believe this is the side of us, buried in the sub-conscious that tends to surface in times of crisis, particularly when one confronts mortality in himself or one of his loved ones.

In the dynamics of family relationships in times of crisis, and as a direct result of each member's "confrontation" with his total inner self, we see new aspects of the personality emerge. The public persona, even the one adjusted for family use, is altered to reflect the events of the moment, which have disturbed dramatically the inner equilibrium of the psychic makeup. I'm not suggesting dramatic changes, but much more subtle ones, often displayed more in body language or even in silences than in overt notions. The naturally taciturn does not change into the loquacious one; the more outgoing extroverted one does not suddenly become the introspective one.

From my prior point of view, what struck me most profoundly was one of the subtle changes that occurred. It is hard to describe and it pertains more to the male members of the family: it was the emergence of a feeling, a certain aura of "tenderness" in our interpersonal relationships. It transmitted an unmistakable sense of caring, empathy and love, qualities of human nature that men in our Western culture find extremely difficult to express. Psychologists tell us that we have both masculine and feminine sides to our personality. Perhaps the caring, nurturing aspects of the feminine side of my sons' nature emerged during this experience. My daughter Pat has always displayed this quality of her personality, but it became obvious to me that she has stepped up the tempo a big notch or two.

People cope with adversity in many different ways. At one end of the spectrum the realists confront it head on, facing it squarely with the facts, however grim. At the other end, we find almost total denial, a refusal to look at the facts and a desperate effort to run away from the problem. In the middle, we have the majority who vacillate from one pole to the other but eventually settle on a mindset they can live with.

I am a realist. I want to know all the facts with no dilution of their potential consequences and outcomes. My biggest problem with my family was how frank and open I could be without going beyond the emotional limits they could handle.

Everyone in the family knew the prognosis, which is why I wanted it, but the degree to which this grim knowledge had been assimilated and accepted by them I did not know. It was only through delicate probing in one-on-one conversations that I was able to gauge how far I should go in discussing my condition. When at a certain point in a conversation you find the person taking the first opportunity to leave the room, you know you have passed the line and gone a little beyond the tolerance level. Likewise, when the conversation became strictly one way, a monologue for me, then I knew it was time to back off. Above all, I wanted to reassure each one that I could cope with this disease and hopefully to relieve some of the anxiety and pressure I knew they were experiencing. Gradually, over a period of time I believe we have reached a point where we can realistically discuss my cancer.

In reflecting on family, one of the more touching recollections for me was a gathering of the family at our house the night before I was scheduled for surgery. Everyone was there. It was the first time that everyone had been together since the disclosure of the disease and there was a profound sense of awkwardness in the room. No one really knew what to say and I felt that everyone was looking at me for clues as to what I felt and what they should talk about. The women had segregated themselves in the kitchen and I was alone with 'the guys' – my three sons (Joe, Jack and Mike) and my fifteen-year-old grandson, Kevin. I am close to Kevin as a first grandchild and I had felt sorry for him knowing the ambivalent feelings he was going through and observing that he was near tears during the entire evening.

I finally managed to steer the conversation to the lighter side and humor saved the day. Even in the worst of circumstances, don't ever underestimate the special benefits of humor. It is that unique characteristic of human beings that sets us apart from the animals and gives a great deal of balance and pleasure to life. The guys began to recount reminiscences principally about early family life, which completely broke the spell of doom and gloom, which had pervaded the gathering. I observed Kevin with the freedom to laugh and I felt good, sensing that he was learning a very good lesson on family values and the knowledge that we share all of life's experiences. This was good therapy for the guys who find it so difficult to share their emotions. Fortunately, the women have an innate capacity to "unload" on each other, which enables them to cope much better than men.

Like everything else in life, there is a positive and negative aspect to things. The little family gathering was a very positive experience, to share the love and affections of my family, to enjoy the humor and pathos of the life we had all enjoyed and to know that I had great resources behind me regardless of what the future would bring. But it was also a bittersweet experience. It had its dark side. Family life is so intimate you just don't want to leave it. You are losing a precious part of "you" and regardless of how strong your beliefs are in the afterlife and the continuity of life with those you love as well as with those who have preceded you, you feel sadness and pain at the prospect. The unknown by any standard is an awesome thing to face.

CHAPTER IV: THE MIND OF MODERN MEDICINE

The world of modern medicine was mysterious to me prior to my illness. True enough, when friends and acquaintances had contracted one of the more serious illnesses, some of their relatives would indulge their fascination to explain in detail the esoteric medicines and therapies they were being subjected to. Sometimes it sounded almost inhumane, the extent to which modern medicine would go to burn you, cut you, eliminate or replace body parts and literally tear you apart to keep you alive. I regarded much of this as gross exaggeration and the tendency of human nature to highlight the bizarre and dramatic aspects of life. My indoctrination into the work of chemotherapy and radiation soon gave me a fresh viewpoint.

It's been almost three months since my operation and the doctors felt I had regained my strength and I was ready to begin the pre-scheduled program of chemotherapy and radiation. The first part of the program consisted of five consecutive days of injections, to be followed by three weeks of rest, to allow the system to recover from chemo's heavy assault on the immune system. Considering the fact that the chemicals are literally killing thousands of cells, hopefully bad ones but healthy ones as well, it is little wonder that fatigue began to set in early in the game. Blood count had to be taken each time the chemo was administered and readings taken of white cells, red cells, platelets, and other blood components to ascertain whether they were sufficiently high to tolerate the chemicals. Fortunately, in my case the blood counts held up remarkably well.

Expected side effects from the treatment had not as yet kicked in and I felt reasonably good, so we decided to take a quick trip to the Jersey shore to visit our good friends of thirty years, Harry and Joan. While I felt a certain apprehension in leaving the safe haven of home, it turned out to be a very nice visit and a pleasant interlude from my normal new life.

I must say there is a mystical but melancholy effect that the experience of the ocean has on the person. Facing the ultimate questions in life, Harry and I walked the shoreline until I got tired and it was evident that Harry was doing most of the talking. Harry is one of those rare human beings you are fortunate to have as a friend. He is totally and sincerely compassionate without being maudlin, is never overbearing and takes life as it is given, making the best of where he is – a great guy and a great natural therapist for me.

The physical side of illness is only half the story. After all, we are composed of body and soul and this composite being called man must achieve an internal harmony if he is to be healed. In my spiritual life, I began to find great comfort in many things. Nancy and I began praying together, saying a rosary each night just before going to bed. Since the terrors of the night are always there, ready to surface at any time, I found the late-night prayer to be a soothing and peaceful prelude to sleep, and the benefits of sharing it with someone made it all the more comforting to my troubled mind.

During the day I read extensively, favoring those remarkable books of Bernie Siegel. Combining my reading with Siegel's meditation tapes gave me an opportunity to reflect on my present life in a much more balanced way, allowing my mind to disengage from its heavy emotional moorings and transcend into a brighter atmosphere.

In some ways, I felt I was getting used to my cancer, but from time to time it continued to hit me with full force. I knew I had to develop the ability to live on a day-to-day basis and get what enjoyment I could out of life without torturing myself about tomorrow. This is not an easy thing to do.

The great uncertainty of not knowing when and if the cancer will come back is tough to handle. You try not to think of it and continue to hope and pray for a cure, but deep down you know the odds are not in your favor – too widespread an invasion of the lymph nodes, too many opportunities for random dispersal of microscopic particles through the bloodstream, but I do believe that faith can heal and my hope lies in this direction.

It takes much discipline and a great effort of will to keep things in balance. "Living in the Now" is difficult under normal circumstances, but when your immediate past has a truly awesome specter lurking there with ominous portents for its future course, your "now" is rarely free of both past and present.

Time flies when you're having fun, but strangely enough, time can also fly by when you are combating a strange new illness and coping with the day-to-day surprises you encounter. I am now through almost three months of radiation. I am a Stoic by nature and tend to downplay the vicissitudes of life, perhaps a reflection of my childhood. My mother inculcated that type of mentality into our life and both my brother and sister reflect that same quality of Stoicism. A familiar pattern emerges – keep a proper reserve and a stiff upper lip at all times, abhor weakness, suffer the pain and move right ahead and develop a strong will.

Many years later, as I reflect upon my childhood, I have come to see that mom's program can be very effective in making your life productive, but it has some shortcomings. I became acutely aware that I had built barriers between myself and my fellow men. A certain incipient coldness had developed, choking off some of the spontaneity and fun of life and, to a degree, inhibiting my ability to develop warm and intimate human relationships. The sad part of it is that those warm feelings are there, captured deep inside, only waiting to be expressed and I just haven't found the way to do it consistently.

Chemotherapy is an art form, practiced by individual oncologists. Consider, there are in excess of a hundred chemicals that have been proven effective for certain types of cancer and probably thousands more that have been proven ineffective. Selecting the right combination of chemicals for your type of cancer is left to the judgment of the oncologist and his expertise. He will rely largely on statistics that are available in his specialized field, but also on his personal experience and success rates with his own patients. It is obvious that careful consideration should be given to the selection of the competent and experienced specialist, or preferably a team of experts since we are dealing with a complex and baffling disease.

The chemicals selected for my therapy were 5-FU and Lucavoron. These would be administered in the oncologist's facility, which was adequately equipped with doctor's offices, a small lab for blood work and a comfortable room equipped to handle injections for five patients simultaneously.

What struck me forcefully from my first visit to this facility was the atmosphere of the place. The staff of nurses and technicians was among the most pleasant and accommodating people I've met in the medical community. Not only that, but the patients in the nursing room and those taking injections were congenial, pleasant and very solicitous of your well-being. Amazing, considering that these patients were all very sick people. I guess we realized we were all in the same sinking boat and could take solace in our common plight, but I was delighted with the total absence of doom and gloom. My ever-faithful wife, Nancy, who is a one hundred percent people person, soon got to know most of the regular patients as well as the staff and it became a home away from home for us.

Chemo injections can be administered directly by needle or intravenously. The direct injection in the arm is no problem, so long as they get a good vein. Mine are on the smaller side, so on several occasions I had to sustain the discomfort of several false starts. It only takes the nurse a few minutes to complete the procedure and away you go. The intravenous, slow-drip method which some chemicals require, can take several hours so the patients undergoing treatments usually have some company or listen to tapes, or at least have reading material. All in all, taking chemo injections is not a problem, since there is no discomfort or pain and side effects are not usually felt until sometime afterward. However, I am told that some patients experience nausea on the way home and need the barf bag to forestall disaster.

For me, undergoing chemotherapy was a strange experience. Let's start by considering the dreaded "side effects." Whoever coined the phrase was guilty of a gross misnomer. They are hardly "side effects," in the category of a minor rash, but rather more a direct assault on your body, sometimes rather brutal but always a totally unpleasant experience. I don't want to unduly alarm anyone who is undergoing chemotherapy or radiation, or anticipating this treatment, but I believe in being a realist and telling it like it is, and it ain't pleasant.

To wake up in the middle of the night with a simultaneous attack of nausea or "dry heaves," diarrhea, dry mouth with ulcers and severe stomach cramps, can be a rather debilitating experience. Afraid to leave the "john" and aided and abetted by the presence of a trusty bucket, you persevere and get through the agony, leaving you in a state of exhaustion. I know the description I've given is rather melodramatic but quite consistent with the facts.

Fortunately, there are some anti-nausea and anti-diarrhea medicines that work and these eventually helped ameliorate the problem. Also, the system seems to adjust somewhat to the chemicals and the side effects begin to lessen. Generally, though, I found that for each of the four-week cycles of chemo I underwent, I experienced one tough week, followed by periods of much less discomfort. I must admit that at the conclusion of five months of therapy I made the honest assessment that it was not as bad as I had anticipated.

Looking back on my first experience with chemotherapy and after discussing it with other patients, I have come to the conclusion that much of it is mind over matter. I believe we are bombarded with so many horror stories that we begin our treatment fully expecting to undergo gruesome side effects. Bernie

Siegel had prepared several of his tapes with this problem in mind. These tapes are designed to be listened to just prior to undergoing chemotherapy or radiation or even while receiving the treatment. This technique is probably related to auto-hypnosis or auto-suggestion and I believe it is very helpful to those of us with psycho-somatic tendencies. After all, a system all geared up in tension is not going to respond to a stressful situation as well as one that is calm, cool and collected.

In between periods of active therapy, during the weeks allotted for recovery time to allow the body to replace blood cells and other effects of the chemical radiation onslaught, we took the opportunity to relax a little and get away from it all. We spent several two-or-three-day visits at the shore taking full advantage of the wonderful hospitality of our good friends, Harry and Joan, who are truly Christian people. Since my energy level and stamina were at an all-time low, they kept everything on a low-key basis, giving me much needed quiet time to relax and recuperate. Playing cards at night, enjoying good conversation and fellowship with people who care for each other is pretty good therapy for anyone and I am certainly grateful for my share of it at Harry and Joan's.

I am going to digress a little from the medical or physical aspects of the story and move into the area of spirituality. I make no apologies for the change of pace since this book is all about a journey, a journey with cancer, and a very substantial part of that journey was a spiritual re-awakening for me with deep insights into my life that never occurred before. This part of the story is very special for me and one I hope I share with someone who wants to believe, who wants to touch reality at its very core. This is the story of Helen and Steve.

I was not a close friend of Helen and Steve. My wife had developed a close friendship with Helen ten years ago, when she became active in the Charismatic movement. We did not socialize. Nancy had kept me abreast of her experience with the Charismatics and it began to impress me how much her life was changing as a direct result of her exposure to this group. Her prayer life was blossoming, her compassion for others gaining and a general peacefulness was becoming an integral part of her personality. I was impressed! I knew she was proselytizing for my benefit but in a most subtle way.

After several years, I accompanied her to a Charismatic meeting. How did I react to my first meeting at a Charismatic session? I was both shocked and elated by the experience. This was the warmest, most spontaneous and caring group of people I had ever encountered. When a fully-grown man gives you a warm bear-hug, which would be anathema in my Spartan and austere background, you immediately feel highly uncomfortable. But after a few minutes of absolutely warm and spontaneous conversation, on his part, you get the message – this guy is for real. His gracious welcome to me was not an isolated experience. Many of the men and women attending the meeting expressed themselves in the same warm and caring manner. I soon felt less uncomfortable and ceased looking for the nearest quiet corner where I could remain unnoticed. In fact, I felt a good hug might not be a bad idea and had some real potential for warming the heart.

The service began, led by several lay people who were thoroughly grounded in the Charismatic movement. I am not sure service is the right word to describe the proceedings. It was more of a prayer exercise directed by the aforementioned leaders and participated in freely and spontaneously by the group who seemed to join in whenever the "Spirit moved them." Then, I was startled by the swelling sound of many voices engaged in the major charisma called glossolalia, which is better known as "speaking in tongues." This cacophony of sounds had no cohesive or understandable language or meaning, it was simply sound, the humming mixture of voices in varied tempos and rhythm patterns. Quite frankly, I was intimidated and very uncomfortable, even though my life partner was enthusiastically verbalizing her special gift of tongues.

I don't want to dwell on the nature of speaking in tongues, since I am hardly knowledgeable enough to convey its true meaning and place in religious practices. Suffice it to say that the practice is well authenticated in scripture as evidenced by Paul in his various letters and affirmed vigorously by the Early Christian Church. Unfortunately, and even in my mind, regrettably, it is given only lukewarm endorsement or practical advocacy by the modern Catholic hierarchy. Perhaps the fear of being accused of superstition in our modern secular culture has even infiltrated the ranks of our hierarchy and intimidated them.

I gradually accepted the fact that speaking in tongues was nothing more than a very special form of praise and prayer given as a special gift to many practicing and devout Christians. While the understanding of this hidden form of language was not comparable to the experience of the apostles after the descent of the Holy Spirit, when the multitude with all their diverse languages were thunderstruck and when the apostles spoke to them in a "tongue" that each understood perfectly. It, nonetheless, has historical biblical roots emanating from this incredible experience.

Some people are also given the gift of "interpretation" of tongues, and at the meetings I attended, such interpretations were freely given, many in the form of messages and insights coming through the presence of the Holy Spirit. In the final analysis, public prayer and intimate sharing of prayers answered is at the heart of these spiritual communities. Someday, the members of our large body of church members may overcome the sophistication of modern culture and return to the simple beauty of intimate community worship and praise as practiced by the early church.

At the very beginning of my first week of therapy I had an unusual and completely unexpected visit. It was Helen and Steve who had just arrived from Florida to visit their daughter. I doubt whether Helen and Steve had ever been in our house before, so I was sort of taken back at their presence at my front door, all tanned and glowing, and exuding their usual enthusiasm for life. I must admit it had not been one of my better days and I spent the better part of it buried in a chair, scraping the bottom and feeling sorry for myself. Helen and Steve's visit proved to be a marvelous elixir, a pick-me-up that brought me to life again, in a truly big way.

After an hour of pleasant conversation, Helen suggested that she would like to pray over me and asked Steve and Nancy to join her. She has a profound gift of prayer, absolutely beautiful in its scriptural sources and made especially meaningful by her ability to personalize her prayers to meet the special needs of the person being prayed for. While I remained seated in my chair, Helen, Steve and Nancy stood over me with their hands resting on my head while Helen prayed over me. The "laying on of hands" was a beautiful and moving experience for me and, surprisingly, I did not feel the least bit uncomfortable, even with the use of "tongues."

After several minutes of beautiful prayers, which moved me emotionally, I began to feel a peculiar warmth or glow which I could accurately describe as a "wave of heat" begin at my head and gradually permeate my entire body. Was it simply an illusion, a physical manifestation of a highly emotional experience I was subject to, or, something different, touching the spiritual and numinous range of reality? I don't know.

I can attest to several things of which I am certain. This was unlike any experience I had ever felt in my life and that includes a few ecstatic spiritual experiences I had in my early twenties when I was deeply engrossed in and fascinated by Thomistic philosophy and the influence of the mystics.

The other key factor is that my basic personality is generally not responsive to highly emotional influences, and in fact, is generally repulsed by ostentatious open displays of raw emotion. My reaction that day was completely contrary to my character and it astounded me.

I'm not that knowledgeable in the area of serendipity or synchronicity, those esoteric realms of the human psyche that the eminent psychiatrist Carl Jung, has waded through and validated. However, a strange coincidence attended my first visit from Helen. Several weeks prior to Helen's arrival I had come across an amazing little book by Agnes Sanford entitled "The Healing Light." The book recounted numerous healing experiences she had in her life and gave many anecdotal stories of the power of these serendipitous happenings. She recounted her positive belief in the efficacy and power of "the laying on of hands" which was practiced extensively in her charismatic ministry.

Was the discovery of the Agnes Sanford book a pure coincidence, or was there a hidden meaning in its unearthing at this point in time? Perhaps. But it was another strange coincidence. That book had been buried in an obscure drawer for probably ten years and belonged to my wife who had purchased it at a Charismatic meeting she attended with Helen. Looking for something else, I had come across it in a place I never go into, found it, and somehow got absorbed in it.

After completing the book and re-reading several sections, I was truly impressed with her strong faith in the visitation of the Spirit in human affairs, particularly in the special healing powers given to people of strong faith. I remember saying to myself: there is only one person in this world I could think of whom I would like to pray over me with the "healing touch" and that would be Helen. Never did I dream that two weeks later Helen would pop up in my house, 1,500 miles from her home, and would be praying over me. Another coincidence? Perhaps, but I interpret it in a radically different way.

I am convinced that Helen's visit and Agnes Sanford's little book were special gifts to me and are not accidental happenings. I think the Lord was looking out for me, my special needs, and gave me a unique gift of his grace. Agnes Sanford came into my life out of the distant past and Helen was the facilitator and bearer of gifts the Lord decided to bestow on me. Like anything else in life, we are "Doubting Thomas's" by nature and faith is sometimes a tenuous quality. I wish my faith were always so strong that there never would be doubt, but then I would be less than human and I would forego the hat of freedom which is the crowning point of man's humanity and his ultimate glory. As the gospel explains it: "I have faith, oh Lord, but help what little faith I have." Nothing much has changed in that regard in 2000 years.

By mid-July I had finished my course in radiation therapy and was getting ready for the next round of chemotherapy. I needed several weeks of rest to recover from the punishment of all that powerful energy flowing through my body leaving a residue, which would take weeks to dissipate. Extreme fatigue had set in and at times it was an effort to just lift my arms. I spent many hours in a chaise lounge soaking up the sun and not having the energy to move. I was reminded of St. Francis of Assisi with his beautiful poem to "Brother Sun" which complemented his ode to Sister Moon, Mother Earth and Sister Star. That holy man could not get over the ecstasy of marveling at God's glorious creation and its real affinity to mankind. As Shakespeare phrased it: "One bough of nature makes the whole world kin."

My appetite was poor. The chemo had literally destroyed the taste buds in my mouth and everything tasted like cotton candy or plastic foam. The only exception seemed to be fruit juices where the citric acid was strong enough to titillate the few remaining taste buds. Coupled with my limited stomach capacity, the absence of taste and appetite played havoc with my weight and I soon dropped down to 140 pounds, about 35 pounds below my normal weight and still falling. Quite a few more pounds would slip away before this disease had run its course. All in all, aside from the daily trips to the hospital, the radiation program was tolerable, and I survived it. The staff at Abington was excellent, a very competent professional organization that I was quite happy with.

Thinking ahead, I began to anticipate the tension that the month of October would bring. All of the chemotherapy and the radiation would have been completed and a battery of tests would be given to ascertain whether the cancer had metastasized or re-occurred in the stomach and esophagus. The tension and build-up to that time was very difficult to control. Living in the "now" is a very sound philosophy and the techniques I had employed had worked very well – prayer, tapes, meditation and carefully selected reading. But now comes the big question, had all this grueling therapy worked or was the "Big C" alive and well in my body?

My oldest son Joe may have surmised the growing anxiety and suggested he and I take a trip to the West Coast. He had a seminar in San Francisco that occupied his time for several days and by extending his time a few more days we could leisurely drive that glorious coastline down to Monterey. I hesitated at first but Nancy strongly urged I take the trip, so off we flew.

The trip turned out to be wonderful therapy for me. We stayed at a beautiful and gracious old hotel. We even enjoyed the "English Tea" we attended in late afternoon in a delightful reception room. Here scones and finger sandwiches were served on exquisite china complemented by a beautiful silver service. The English do seem to have a civilized way of enjoying life.

The first few mornings I had the luxury of staying in bed and enjoying breakfast in our room while Joe went off to meetings. The afternoon and evenings we spent together, enjoying dinner – in my limited way – which gave us the opportunity to enjoy some nice conversation.

Funny thing about difficult problems, we can only tolerate a certain amount of conversation or an inevitable tension sets in, and discussing the possibility of the imminent death of a loved one does not blend in well with relaxed dinner conversation. Here the mutual acceptance of benign and comforting silence is the best antidote available. It is a well-known quality of human nature that silence can result in a beautiful form of non-verbal communication and can be just as effective as words in exchanging empathy and compassion. It is the language I am trying to learn.

The California coast is truly magnificent, one of the wonders of nature. Joe rented a little Ford Mustang convertible and we soaked in the beauty of that coastline, luxuriating in the warm sun and stopping at every good vantage point where the scenery was particularly appealing. We even took the opportunity to sit on a deserted beach with a rugged rocky backdrop and confront head-on the huge waves breaking directly in front of us. Simply awesome. Big Sur, Carmel and finally Monterey for several leisurely enjoyable days and finally back to San Francisco and to the flight to Philadelphia. This wonderful interlude had taken the tension and anticipation away and I am grateful to this day for Joe's very considerate reading of a difficult situation.

REMEMBERING MOMENTS IN A LIFE

John displays a knowing smile wearing the 'Pig Shirt,' named for its bright pink hue. It was the only T-shirt he ever owned, given by his family in jest. Photo taken in late 1994, during remission, outside his Holland, PA home.

JPR Solo

John enjoys the beach at Big Sur, California in 1992.
This stop was part of a drive along the Pacific Coast
Highway with Joe, his eldest son.

Cancer took 35 pounds from John after his first surgery. Surgeons
removed a portion of his stomach, and ongoing chemotherapy damaged
his taste buds, dampening his appetite. Seen here, a large smile still
dominates his drawn face in 1992.

Starting Out: North Catholic High School

Hands in the dirt, or on a violin–some days within minutes of each other–if football and orchestra practices ran consecutively. John participated in a number of extra-curriculars in high school.

Starting Out–continued
(photos from his 1949 college year book)

Philosophy Club

The La Salle Philosophy Club is a new organization on the campus investigating the concepts of great thinkers of all time. In weekly informal discussions of philosophic writings its members have developed a deeper appreciation of the significant factors of life, devoid of superficiality.

It is dedicated to the proposition that Plato, Aristotle, Saint Thomas Aquinas, Saint Augustine, and the other "lovers of wisdom" solved their problems with a fundamental logic that is of value in solving the problems of the modern world.

John's deep and lifelong interest in philosophy took root in the Philosophy Club at LaSalle.

He also found his leadership voice at LaSalle as Senior Class President (sitting front right) and as a member of the Student Council. He earned all A's that year as well.

Starting Out – continued

John and Nancy at
the LaSalle Harvest
Dance in 1949.

John and Nancy, recently engaged, on
the Atlantic City boardwalk. 1950's
dress protocol: a suit and tie for men;
a suit for women, complete with hat,
gloves and high heels.

The couple leaving church
after their wedding, and
later posing for an Easter
photo on the front lawn of
their first home.

Twice Young

As a young father: John with his completed family - three sons and a young daughter, approximately four or five years old, standing outside of Assumption BVM Church, circa 1961-62. Two other photos from roughly the same period, show Michael, Patty, and Jack at a baseball game with John, and all three boys (eldest to youngest) Joe, Michael and John Junior (Jack) at the beach with their dad.

As a young grandfather: John, 57, teaches his oldest grandchild, Kevin (age 7) how to raise the flag at the family vacation spot in Avalon, NJ in 1984.

Photos With Nancy During His Journey With Cancer

John and Nancy, during his 39-month journey with cancer.
During the ups and downs of John's illness, the couple
posed for photos in many locations:
Outside a home in Florida, inside and outside their
home in Holland, PA, and at John's 65th birthday party.

A day of grace: In remission, under a bright
sun, John and Nancy revel in a day at the
beach in Wildwood, NJ 1994.

Work – Horn & Hardart

The college class president became a senior executive in his mid 30s with Horn and Hardart, a pioneer in automat food services, shown below.

Published by the Horn & Hardart Baking Company, Philadelphia, Pa. • Vol. 1, No. 1 • November, 1968

HORN & HARDART ON THE MOVE

Speakers shown above joined in introducing company's new plans. (Left to right) Jerome B. Gray, Thacher Longstreth, David S. Roberts, James D. Cannon, John P. Ryan.

As a director of the firm, John was featured prominently in company promotions, in print and in public.

Work – Seafood America

Later in life (his mid-50s) John and his brother Bob, shown here, opened a restaurant—Seafood America. John worked long hours in the kitchen and made his faith known to his employees via a cross on the wall in the food preparation area. On sunny days, he often stopped work to watch the sun set and urged the kitchen staff to step outside with him.

During this time, married and work life merged, as Nancy and John worked long hours together in the restaurant.

JPR's 65th Birthday Party

A significant high point in John's days of remission: all three generations of his family, along with his brother and sister, and numerous friends, celebrated his 65th birthday. Shown here, John looks straight into the camera, focused on his role as patriarch.

California Trip, 1992

John and his oldest child, Joe, on the beach at Big Sur, repeating a theme that is almost as old as the family.

Remission: Wildwood Beach and Photo with Pat

John described the moments after he and Nancy received formal notice of his remission: "Nancy and I literally danced around the room at the good news, a spontaneous outburst from me, which was completely out of character for my reserved personality." Once that news was out it seemed like the cameras came out too. We see John and Patty sitting in front of the flower garden at John's house; John on the beach in New Jersey; John and Nancy at the beach during a visit to Florida.

JPR's Book and Journals

John's planning and writing of the book were done with pen and paper. The photo here shows his original outline, with subsequent notes for a work in progress, undertaken in the final months of his life.

The Power of Journaling: John also kept a private journal during his 39-month journey with cancer. Shown here, enlarged to a size that allows us to enter his world, is a one-page sample. He encouraged those with serious illnesses to try this method of sense making. "Journal writing and meditation have proven to be excellent therapies for people trying to get hold of their lives. I urge the reader to try them."

Memorial Bench

How do you summarize the life of a man like John Ryan? His strong will to move forward in most of what he did pushed his thoughts and actions into many of life's arenas. How much more challenging it was for his family to capture his essence in the space of a small plaque on a memorial bench in Chestnut Hill, Philadelphia. The words shown here are a noble attempt to do the impossible. To paraphrase some words from his memoir, John was "all this and more."

This Man's Legacy

John and Nancy, robust, in early adulthood, with four young children, take their version of an iconic American photo during the 1950s: Everyone in their Easter Best on the family lawn.

Like a river of time, John's 'eternal now' moved along, carrying his children to where he and Nancy had been—young adults with children of their own, the cycle of life repeating. Shown below, the children and grandchildren of John and Nancy, the legacy of love and intentional parenting, reaching to a third generation.

CHAPTER V: RESURRECTION: A NEW LIFE

Praise the Lord! Hallelujah! Life is Beautiful!

We received the news from Dr. Spiritos today. "All tests were fine, no evidence of cancer anywhere. You are in a state of remission." You can't imagine the joy, the ecstasy that comes over you at a time like this. You have been given a reprieve, a gift of life, and suddenly the world has been renewed and you are whole again.

I thanked God for this best of all possible news. I could not predict the future, for now I was whole again and my prayers had been answered. Let tomorrow come and bring with it what God wills and I will accept it, secure in the knowledge that He will take care of me. Did He not say that He would take care of us as if we're little children, and that unless we became "like little children we could not enter the Kingdom of Heaven." I was happy and secure to be a child of God.

Nancy and I literally danced around the room at the good news, a spontaneous outburst from me, which was completely out of character for my reserved personality. Nancy, to her credit, has no problem letting her feelings out, and carries everyone along with her. But after so many months of apprehension and tension, suddenly find yourself free again, what a celebration that calls for. We could hardly wait to spread the good news.

Needless to say, that as we made the rounds of family, everyone was ecstatic. It's such a wonderful feeling to know how much you are loved and the integral part you play in family life. We finally completed the family network and got in touch with our close friends who were every bit as ecstatic as had been the family. They had been so generous in spirit, in sharing the pain of the last year and now they were equally as generous in sharing the joy. Good friends are one of life's great blessings and attest so well to the scriptural imperative that we are "our brothers' keeper."

It was now late November, on the doorstep of Thanksgiving and Christmas, the best of all possible times to receive good news. Being "cancer free," I could now look forward with peace of mind to the holidays, secure in the knowledge that doctors, hospitals and therapists were behind me. A routine oncologist visit was scheduled for January. I had made up my mind to enjoy every day to the fullest and let the future take care of itself. As Jesus told us in the gospel, "Fear is useless, what is needed is trust." I trust the Lord, more so every day, and am quite content to place my future in His hands. My illness truly brought me this gift of peace.

In retrospect, 1993 was a quite normal year. With the cancer under control and no scheduled therapies we could resume, or more correctly, begin the life-style of the retired couple. We had been literally forced into an unanticipated retirement as a result of my illness.

Life never seems to be stable for long. At every turn we require adjustments – family relations, business problems, health problems, retirement, and financial realities – all of which can produce their share of tensions and frustrations. Flexibility and adaptability are essential components of a personality today, particularly in a culture with no respect for fixed, stable value systems which gave us such strong foundations in the past.

It is amazing to me, as a result of my illness, how I saw aspects of human nature I had not been aware of before, particularly through the microcosm of my own family. The strong ones step forward and "take charge," while the emotional ones find the means to go beyond their visceral, emotional responses and find a controlled mode of action that allows them to handle traumatic experiences in a mature way. This flexibility surprised me and made things much easier to handle.

I have no better example of someone stepping forward, taking charge and leading the parade than my oldest son, Joe, who became the major-domo and ran the show. I'm sure there were some tensions arising out of the family meetings Joe had been holding with Jack, Mike and Patti that I was not aware of, but they collectively worked it out.

One thing I became painfully aware of is how difficult it is to let go of the control of important aspects of your practical life and allow someone else to make the decisions. I realize now how important it is to accept that help with gratitude and love. It doesn't come easy.

Joe seemed to have a premonition that restlessness might set in as we steered our way into the retired life, and before I could think much about it we had airline tickets to Florida for March. A nice condominium, car rental, dinner money and everything needed for a relaxed week in the Florida sunshine. Needless to say, we had no problem acquiescing to such a splendid arrangement and Nancy and I were off to Florida. We had a totally relaxing trip, plenty of rest time, glorious sunsets, excellent accommodations and a peaceful sojourn in the sun, just what the doctor ordered. We came home well tanned, rested and optimistic about what lay ahead of us.

The need for constant adjustments in our life present challenges we never dreamed of. Yes, we can plan our life to a certain degree, but the moment we think we have it all together, Whamo! Something pops up out of the blue and we have to redesign the whole package. Unfortunately, it is synergistic and inter-related to a large degree. We all play the "pillow game" every time we punch down one section, up pops another and we just can't get it right. So it is with life, it just won't stay fluffed up just right, too many bumps and hollows to straighten out.

This book deals with one man's journey with cancer, so the reader might legitimately ask: "What does the need for adjustments in life have to do with cancer?" Plenty. Once a person has been given a verdict of cancer, advance stage, the whole life strategy comes to the fore. Every element of one's life demands immediate attention – family, business, social, financial – and your mind begins to enter chaos, everything popping up at once, led of course by the grim specter of the cancer itself.

We all know what we should do in planning our life, at least in the area of financial and retirement planning, but many of us simply fail to do an adequate job. Unfortunately, I ended up in this category and found myself in deep financial problems precisely at the time when the cancer hit.

A brief background might clarify the problem. As a senior executive in a food service company with eighteen years of service, I found myself unceremoniously dumped on the open market with a group of other senior executives as a direct result of a nasty corporate takeover. Ostensibly, my position had seemed solid as a rock and I had been anticipating retirement in five years, under attractive financial arrangements.

I had an interest in a small family restaurant operation and made the decision to try my hand at direct, "hands on" operation of that business. Running completely contrary to the rules of good financial planning, I had also bought out a similar operation at a bargain price where you simply "could not lose." Both decisions were terrible. I had sold the last business acquired at a substantial loss and was "hanging on" in a losing venture on the original operation. We could not sell. The market was saturated and our financial statements were dismal. Then cancer struck and everything turned upside down.

An interesting and important point should be considered here. What effect did my traumatic and chaotic personal business problems have in developing this cancer? Was this the dividend I had received? This is not an idle and groundless speculation. There is a growing body of evidence to support the theory that stress is a causative factor in illness, particularly where the gastro-intestinal system is involved. My cancer had developed in the upper section of my stomach and had invaded the esophagus extensively. An ulcer had

developed prior to the change into cancer, but unfortunately there were no significant symptoms early on when such knowledge could have been extremely beneficial. The only way that cancer could have been detected earlier would have been an endoscopic probe into the area, a procedure that is not routinely done in the annual physical examination.

Back to the grim scenario I found myself confronting in February 1992. I had cancer, was literally broke, having dumped most of my life savings into two failed businesses, was underinsured, and deeply concerned with my wife's future, since she was the typical 50's "housewife" who had done yeoman service in raising her family, but who was hardly qualified to jump into the world of business to support herself should that become necessary. I was in a state of near panic. I could think of little else than the problems and I saw no easy solution. I could not handle it.

Joe could surmise the facts but I believe he was genuinely surprised at the scope of the serious financial problems I had. Such things are usually underplayed by guys like me. Fortunately, and by the grace of God, I had the right guy in my corner. Joe literally took me completely out of my personal and business financial activities. My brother Bob, who was a partner in the business, joined with Joe to direct the business and attempt to negotiate a sale. Within a matter of a few weeks the business was sold. Joe cleared up the tangled personal financial problems and gradually things were under control.

Joe and the other family members had put their skill and their hearts together and relieved me of all the stressful things I was fighting. They gave their mother a rock-like secure base to hang onto in the tough months ahead. What a blessing that was for me. My instructions were very simple: "Forget everything else; we want you to devote one hundred percent of your energy to getting better." I surprised myself by surrendering my ego and false pride and accepted this wonderful gift of love. What better therapy could anyone have come up with?

Therapy can take many forms. Having time on my hands for things I never had time for before, I began to do many little things that were different, a change of pace for me. I spent more time in meditation and prayer. I began to take copious notes of everything I was reading, a practice that I felt put me to the test of whether I was getting anything out of the extensive body of material I was covering. I concluded that it was an excellent discipline if you wanted to gain knowledge. Not only that, but it allowed you to enter into a veritable dialogue or conversation with the author, and get to "know" him. I have read a number of books by Henri Nouwen, a favorite spiritual writer of mine. I've shared his agonies and ecstasies, his hopes and despair and his continuing struggle to be the Christian he wants to be. He opens himself up, makes himself vulnerable in his humanity. He is now a "friend" and I love the man.

I am now deep in a journal covering the changing landscape of my spiritual life. I wish I had started thirty years ago. What I wouldn't give now to read my journal of 1948 – 50, a period in my life where I was in a deep philosophical struggle with myself to answer in a young man's impatient style the deep angst I was trying to overcome.

Comparing that mindset to the more balanced mature mindset of a man with forty-five more years of life experience would, indeed, be fascinating. You simply cannot reconstruct an authentic replica of that mind at that time in history; it has merged too many life experiences into what it is today.

Journal writing, and meditation have proven to be excellent therapies for millions of people trying to get hold of their lives, particularly those who are facing life's most important questions, as a result of serious illness. I would strongly urge the reader, based upon my own experience, to give it a try. It can be very rewarding.

At the risk of being accused of moving into the esoteric fringes of life, I managed to play around with another area, dream analysis. After reading John

Sanford and Morton Kelsey, both highly reputable people, I was encouraged to at least get a little more familiar with dreams and their significance. I was surprised to find out just how significant a role dreams played in the biblical story of God's communication with man. There are still today a substantial number of people who believe that God communicates with man through his dreams. I felt my dreams might give me an insight into the origin of my cancer.

During most of 1993, I kept a detailed record of my nightly dreams and managed to accumulate well over a hundred detailed dream experiences, I'm now in the process of trying to categorize the contents in order to discern meaningful patterns. I do not have the background and training to carry this very far and in the depth to which Jungian psychologists go to interpret the common symbolism of dreams, the so-called archetypes.

What have I learned from my dreams? I guess the thing that surprised me most was the fact that most of my dreams are "old dreams," going back to the period of 1960 to 1980 – very little before and very little after. What have I repressed? Another surprising finding was that ninety percent of those dreams were work related. Had my priorities in life been all screwed up? And a surprising final conclusion, there was a tremendous amount of tension, anxiety and sometimes terror – I was frequently lost.

What possible relationship is there between the onset of cancer and the contents of my dreams? I think there may be a direct, causal relationship. Although the scientific and medical community may disagree with this, (not all of them), I am convinced that my cancer was a direct result of tension and stress built up over many years, culminating in a dramatic breakthrough during the last several years of my business problems. Compounding this is the suggestion that my priorities were wrong – I had put too much emphasis on work and neglected other areas that would have given my life a better balance. I couldn't imagine a contemplative monk leading his simple life ever ending up with my case.

As a result of my dream experiences I am certain of one thing – I never had any relationship with the Divine, nothing numinous or otherworldly. I seemed to be far too engrossed in untangling my own life to worry about another one.

However, those dreams, particularly in a series or group, experienced over many months do give you a composite picture, which I found to be troublesome. Maybe there is a very important message the Lord is trying to give me which has not yet unfolded. I intend to follow my dream life afresh, now that I have become acclimated to what to expect.

So much has been written today with regard to pursuing the so-called "inner life," to find out the real you, the true reality of your being. The majority of people feel confrontation with the inner self like it was the plague. They simply fear the solitude, the oppressive quiet zone, what John S. Dunne calls the "solitude wrapped in silence." Rather, they prefer a busy mind protected by a cacophony of sound – anything to distract.

The inner life can be awesome in many ways; after all it is one small entity, a minute particle of consciousness pitted against the infinite consciousness of the universe, spilling like a small stream into the infinite consciousness, which is God. In facing death, man ultimately will face death alone regardless of who is with him. It is in that "solitude wrapped in silence" that he will meet his maker.

There was a popular television series that showed the lives of the rich and the famous. It was an expression of pure hedonism in an age of pure squander of the mind and "soul" of man. While it may titillate and paint the beautiful life in the fast lane as the ideal for modern man, in reality, it was pathetic, all the pretty people wearing themselves out in a frantic effort to escape the silence, to escape the dreaded solitude, which threatens them.

Rather than following the lives of the rich and famous, I found peace and solace in following the lives of the simple and the tender-hearted, those rare souls who saw life as a gift of love to be shared and given back to one's fellow men. These are the people who had peace in their hearts and were not afraid to spread the joy it brings. They had learned to surrender the self, to give up the ego, and accept the life God had given them. For those who suffer, they are the true heroes to emulate. They lead us to the ways of peace where "fear is useless and trust is found."

The tempo of life through most of 1993 established itself almost without direction, with only routine periodic visits to the oncologist; life seemed to move a little further away from medical influence every month. With my weight improving and my general physical stamina returning, I began to lead a somewhat normal life, even taking on a small part-time job.

Visits to the shore, a broader social life, all contributed to make life better, then in the fall, around Halloween, I remember having a funny feeling that all was not right, nothing tangible, just an intuition my body had that gave that vague message. I assigned it to the normal apprehension that comes and goes with this disease, when you never know for sure when and if the cancer will return. The holidays came, I was feeling good, my doctor visits were favorable and everything seemed in order. They year ended on a happy note and I thanked God for a beautiful year of life I didn't expect to live.

We managed to slip away to Florida in March with Lucy and Joe, close friends of many years. It was a delightful trip with glorious weather, complemented by excellent facilities. Joe's brother had a beautiful house in Coral Gables, which he graciously let us use. Unfortunately, my time was spoiled by a recurring and severe arthritic type pain in my left arm. It would come and go but it was intense and kept me in a state of discomfort through most of the trip. I would have to check on this when I got home. The last thing I needed now was to combat arthritis and go through that agony.

When we arrived home, I set up an appointment with my doctor and she suggested a bone scan and a visit to an ear, nose and throat specialist since I was also complaining of a persistent hoarseness which antibiotics had been unable to cure. We met with Dr. Welsh and he conducted a scope of the throat, esophagus and upper part of the stomach. He was also concerned about the bone scan and managed to have a copy faxed to him from the hospital.

When he came back into the office again I could sense the change in demeanor. Dr. Welsh, an older and well-respected specialist is known to be a blunt man. He lived up to his reputation. He referred me back to my oncologist. He gave me the bad news – an obstruction in the vocal chords and a deterioration of bone in the left arm. The cancer was back!

CHAPTER VI: ARMAGEDDON REVISITED

For me, the agony in the garden is the most poignant and sorrowful part of the Crucifixion story. It touches the chords of my heart that truly devastate me. Christ, the Son of God, the creator of the universe is reduced to a frightened, terror-filled human being begging His father for surcease to an impending, horror-filled doom. He desperately reaches out for human solace but his most trusted disciples are asleep, oblivious of His agony. Back and forth he goes only to find them useless to his needs. Thrice He appeals to His father but to no avail. God and man have abandoned him. He sweats blood.

I had experienced my agony in the garden two years ago and it was a traumatic, devastating experience to taste a chalice of bitterness and hopelessness, which God would not take away from me. Here I am again – Armageddon revisited – going through that same agony of doubt and fear. Thank God, the terrors of the night were not the same, the God of Peace had given me His Peace two years ago in a lonely hospital room and it has never really left me. True, our human nature is weak, belief and hope come hard at times and we continually fight the battle, but God is with us and we survive.

To confirm Dr. Welsh's preliminary diagnosis, the doctors needed another battery of tests--cat scans, bone scans, blood work, x-rays, etc. We had already made arrangements to have them finished a week prior to our meeting with Dr. Spiritos so that we could have a definitive consultation to get the complete story. We were always clutching at straws, perhaps the cancer was not as widespread as the x-rays indicated, and possibly it was localized enough to be controlled. Perhaps chemotherapy and additional radiation would suffice.

Life is a waiting game for those of us enduring a serious illness. We are always in a state of anxiety waiting for those marvelous tools of modern medicine and science to chart our images, to render their cold and dispassionate diagnoses – shadows, hot spots, lesions. Those days of waiting for results are very difficult. No matter how involved you try to become in mundane things, your frenetic mind churns away sorting out possibilities, alternatives and all manner of diverse things. Thoughts just pop in and out of your head willy-nilly. What a magnificent workhorse the human mind is, in all its complexity, if only we could control it.

I had several very difficult nights waiting for test results. In addition, my left arm was now giving me more continuous pain. It stretched from the shoulder to the elbow, and seemed to be embedded deep in the bone. I also had a very tender, painful spot in the center of my back which prevented me from lying prone face-up. Since I could not lie on my side because of the sore arm, I was restricted now to lying in a recliner chair, with my upper body raised.

Sleep came grudgingly, if at all, and I found myself once again in the stillness of the night with plenty of think-time on my hands. Why does the night produce such a fearful and ominous presence at times, and yet at other times it induces a state of euphoria, near ecstasy, like when one gazes at a star-filled sky or feels bathed in the soft moonlight? Perhaps when the earth sleeps and the noise and chatter of the day disappear, the mind can stop and reflect. It can find out once again in the stillness of the night its place in the world. Perhaps peaceful sleep comes from affirmation of life, commitment to once again accept life and to live it as the Lord intended – with joy and gratitude for His gift of creation. The mind is then at rest and peace.

But what about those other nights when the mind is not at rest, where peace seems far away and an agony of doubt and fear begin to color your landscape. I began to experience such nights when sleep would not come and the long, still hours of the night passed slowly by. A tumultuous flood of questions arose spontaneously, seemingly under no conscious control. Questions with no answers, fruitless probing of the mind, producing nothing except frustration and hopelessness. Faith and trust do not leave you at such times. They recede into a deeper level and what emerges is your human weakness and frailty.

On sleepless nights, there seems to be no alternative but to let your mind suffer its self-made torment and wear itself out. Finally, I was able to reach down deep inside and bring back the peace that had been given me and gradually reach a state of rest. Prayer is a road to accepting your fate. It's a tough, hard road, but the only one that works and allows you to live your life, no matter how hopeless it may seem at the time. You accept. You put your trust in the Lord and you find peace and rest – a simple formula, but so hard to achieve.

All the tests were completed and we had our conference with Dr. Spiritos. I knew deep down that the results would be bad or worse, with no steps in between. The diagnosis was worse, way down on the scale. The cancer had metastasized over a wide area. It had developed extensively in the bone in the upper left arm with some indication of cancer in the right leg, the back, and the right lung, which was partially collapsed.

During that visit I also learned that a lymph node removed from my right arm the previous week was malignant. The pathology report indicated it was stomach cancer and not the development of a new cancer. The doctors were amazed that the stomach cancer had metastasized into the upper body area and the bones. This is unusual. Usually stomach cancer spreads into the liver or kidneys. Regardless, we had an extensive intrusion of stomach cancer into multiple areas which precluded the possibility of a "cure." This was made crystal clear to me by Dr. Spiritos who didn't pull any punches. He said the diagnosis was extremely poor and we're talking four or five months of life, possibly a year at the outside.

Time frames in situations of this kind are always shocking. You never get used to them. He indicated the only thing they could offer me was palliative treatment, making me as comfortable and pain-free as possible, and attempting through radiation or chemo to retard or shrink existing tumors. He said, the extensive development of tumors could make that a difficult program to administer.

Fortunately, as in other major conferences with my doctors, my son Joe was with us. This gave much needed support to Nancy and another pair of ears to understand what was being said and its full impact. Sometimes, some of this tends to go over the patient's head or he sees only what he wants to see. Surprisingly, both Nancy and Joe absorbed the grim readings in a reasonable composed way, although it was obvious to me they were both profoundly affected by the extent to which this cancer had developed. We had all been living a little more complacently during the past quiet year.

I have mentioned before how nice it is to have good teamwork with your doctors. While we were still in the office, Dr. Spiritos called Dr. Richter, our radiologist and filled him in on the developments. Dr. Richter's reaction – an expletive or two and the admonition: "Ah shit, I thought we had it licked," an expression of deep disappointment. These doctors are human. They empathize with their patients on a very basic human level. Dr. Richter, in spite of his hectic schedule, wanted us to meet with him that same afternoon.

When we met with Dr. Richter he had examined all of the images and showed us the areas that were affected. He explained possible radiation treatments. He indicated the area in the chest was bad. All the vital organs were clustered together, like traffic on Broad Street, which made it extremely critical to direct powerful energy into these sensitive areas. Without exact measurements, life-sustaining organs could easily be burned. He felt a radiation program would reduce arm pain and targeting the sensitive chest area might help shrink tumors and reduce the discomfort in the back, which would allow me to sleep in my bed. We agreed on this and a five-week program of daily treatments was set up.

The mystery and suspense of waiting for test results was, thankfully, now over.

While the findings were very bad indeed, there is some consolation in knowing where you stand. Being in the dark can be pure torture, allowing the mind free reign to cover every speculation under the sun. When the family had the time to reflect on where we stood now, a completely new picture emerged. The past year of euphoria and hope was gone. That never-ending hope of obtaining a "cure" was no longer a possibility. We now had a clearly defined case of terminal cancer with some pretty well established parameters of time. My whole mindset and ways of approaching the problem had to change abruptly. It was a totally new ball game.

The disappointment we all felt at the recurrence of cancer was a palpable reality, but at the same time, there arose in each of us a feeling that we would cope with it, doing our utmost not only to prolong life but to make it meaningful and enjoyable — living in the now, accepting the blessing of the day (and every day has some). We all sensed the need not to give up but to cope as best we could and trust the Lord to watch over us. I was most grateful to the family for this balanced and reasoned response.

Living in the now is easier said than done. Your mind is forever a free agent, going where it wishes, regardless of your feeble efforts to direct it. Unable to sleep in bed because of the extreme discomfort in my back, I was consigned to spending my nights as best I could in the reclining chair. Some of those nights became very troublesome. I had mentioned before that I had started a journal, writing down my thoughts and feelings as I progressed through my illness. I began reading from a journal page written on February 23, five or six weeks before my cancer came back. I was astounded at some of the thoughts expressed then.

Quoting directly from the journal, I was reminiscing that two years had now gone by since the original diagnosis. God had been good to me and had given me the two years of life I had prayed for. I made the following observations: *"No question, two years ago I didn't expect to see this day. I have, and I am grateful. Do I expect to see a few more years? As I think about answering that question I am really ambivalent about it. Something inside me says yes and that is the answer I lean towards, but another part of me says that things are winding down and something will happen to end the story."*

I go on to say *"Perhaps one of those microscopic cancer cells has lodged in the system and found a home and is now developing a virulent colony to kill me off. That's what happened to Giulio. He lasted a year, but then, out of the blue, the cancer cells had their way and took over."*

I was amazed at just how prescient I had been. The picture I had drawn then was exactly what was confirmed five weeks later when the diagnosis was made. A word about Giulio, a good friend of my brother's, whom I had been talking to on a regular basis trying to keep his spirits up. He had developed stomach cancer and was going through the rough spots I had experienced during my first year of treatment. I think I was helpful to him in counseling him as to what to expect as well as some ways of coping with the problem.

Giulio's death shook me quite a bit. He had become a soul mate, a fellow victim and we found it easy to communicate. He had been coming along quite well and the family was encouraged as was Giulio, and then suddenly in a matter of weeks it was all over. The cancer had its way and moved quickly to claim its victim. I prayed for Giulio and tried to reconcile my troubled mind to the grim realities of this disease. It wasn't easy.

After two weeks of radiation with minimal side effects, a minor miracle occurred. The pain in my back suddenly was gone and I could return to my bed and get a good night's sleep. Apparently, the tumors in that area had shrunk to a point where the inflamed nerves were relieved of pressure. What a relief and a blessing. I owed one to Dr. Richter for successfully weaving his way down Broad Street to help remedy this painful situation. The pain in my arm gradually disappeared, with help from morphine. Fortunately, all of these things working together gave me a reasonably comfortable and pain-free lifestyle.

On May 20th the newspaper carried the headline that Jackie Kennedy had died that day of lung cancer. Ordinarily, I would read the headline, maybe read a paragraph or two, and express a note of sadness and move on to other things. But not now. Here is a kindred spirit, a sharer in my humanity, with whom I have a lot in common. I read avidly the story of Jackie Kennedy. I wanted to know all the details. We shared something in common.

When I reflected on Jackie Kennedy, several profound thoughts emerged. Cancer levels the playing field. It respects neither rich nor poor, nor famous nor unknown. Jackie's death also sends another clear message – when your time comes with this disease, all the medical and technical expertise in the land will not save you. You should accept the inevitable, acquiescing to the will of God and, hopefully, die gracefully and in peace.

Finally, the radiation program had been completed. I was very happy to see it end. Week by week it had been exerting its toll on my system. The ending was welcomed indeed. I had suffered a great deal of nausea and could not eat. My weight had gone down to an all-time low, 125 pounds, and my energy level was terrible. It takes about two weeks for the radiation to get out of the system so I looked forward to a return to normal soon. It seems there is always a biblical passage that is appropriate for the occasion and the one that came to me was from II Corinthians. "Though the outer man is falling into decay, the inner man is renewed day by day."

Facing death is not easy. It seems to be a total negation of everything that exists. If that's all there is to this experience of living, it's a total absurdity, a meaningless frolic in an undeniable and limitless cosmos that functions without purpose or end. As I have stated previously, there is no way I can accept this premise.

Life must have meaning; the cosmos must have meaning and behind it all looms large the transcendental PRESENCE that brought it all into being. While we cannot unravel the mystery with our limited intellect we see enough in the natural order of things to show us there is meaning and purpose in life. Knowing the limitations of man's reason, a beneficent and loving Father gave us His self-revelation, and ultimately the gift of His Son to make it crystal clear that life does have meaning and we are not only integral to the meaning, we are the pre-eminent.

CHAPTER VII: LIVING THE ETERNAL NOW

Time is a troublemaker. It is fickle and capricious and at times downright annoying. When you want it to slow down so that you might savor the moment, it races by, and when you want it to pass quickly, it drags on endlessly, driving you to distraction. Time is a physiological phenomenon, in the sense that your body and the world it inhabits is part of a system that moves from point to point in a succession of events that comprise the duration of our lifetime. Time's essence lies in the inner recesses of the mind or soul where existence approaches the eternal. Past merges irreversibly into present and both ultimately become the future. We then, become a constantly changing, evolving, new being whose ultimate end is part of the great mystery where time becomes eternity.

I have done much reading during my illness, searching for therapies, techniques or just practical wisdom that might be helpful to me in achieving peace of mind. Considering the impact this has on your healing potential, knowing that the mind can influence the body's immune system, such a search can be very meaningful.

There is no question that prayer and meditation have been the bedrock resources that have sustained me, but the real sleeper that has loomed large in my coping mechanisms is learning to live in the eternal now.

The eternal now is an elusive quality to acquire and master, since our teeming mind always seems to resist the discipline that is required. We dwell on the past, constantly specu-

late on the future and end up forgetting the potential of the moment, the now. Yet, the now is the only reality. We can only live in the present. We can think about the past, and the future, but we cannot be there. They are mental constructs. But our minds can vacillate between all three, thoroughly diluting if not completely negating the potential joys and pleasures of the present, the now.

How often have you been absorbed by beauty – a landscape, a magnificent sunset or a sublime immersion in great music -- only to let it be stolen from you by your capricious mind which intrudes its past or future into the moment, thoroughly destroying the pleasure that was yours? This is what happens all the time when you choose not to live in the eternal now – when your mind is allowed to run unfettered in the landscape of your consciousness. Yet, with a little practice and control you can live fully in the present with all the possibilities it has to offer and enhance tremendously your peace of mind.

Living in the eternal now, allowing yourself to be completely absorbed in the things that give you pleasure, is available to anyone who has the discipline to achieve it. No matter which path one takes to achieve this state of mind – meditation, prayer, reading, good music, good friends, family gatherings, hobbies, travel, solitary walks, exercise – the end result can be the same, a sense of satisfaction and contentment that you are living your life and enjoying the moment.

You may legitimately say, "easier said than done." Here I am with a terminal illness, not knowing when my time is up and unable to control this apprehension and fear that is always lurking somewhere in my consciousness. Then, there are the times you feel just plain lousy – discomfort from therapy, pain and total fatigue – how does one then embrace that and relish the eternal now? My eternal now, as I write this, positively stinks and it won't go away.

I agree with those who see the apprehension and fear as inescapable. I have experienced these times and "it ain't easy" to dispel them. These feelings are persistent and a very natural reaction to a bad situation. I also know that little by little, as you take the positive approach and learn to discipline your mind and emotions, you will find yourself learning to live more and more in the eternal now and enjoying your life more. Yes, you certainly can allow yourself time to think about the past, particularly when the memories are pleasant, or even to speculate on the future if it serves some practical need and is not just an exercise in morbidity, but the secret is for you to control your mind, don't let it control you. You will eventually surprise yourself as to how much of your life can be pleasurably lived in the eternal now.

It has been several weeks since radiation was completed. We met with Dr. Spiritos to determine our next course of action. It's funny with this cancer game, you are almost driven to do something rather than waiting passively for something to happen. We reviewed the situation in detail and the only option available to me was another attempt to contain the spread of cancer through chemotherapy. Again, Dr. Spiritos indicated this was a "long shot," but said he would give it a chance if I wanted to try. Probably operating on the theory that any course of action was better than no course of action, we set up a ten-week program of chemo, which would take us through the heart of summer and into September. Oh, those hazy, lazy days of summer.

Ten weeks of chemo involves quite a bit of discomfort – stomach cramps, nausea and extreme fatigue. Since the chemo ruined my appetite and the side effects played havoc with my eating pattern, I began to drop in weight, getting down into the 120's. I began to hate to look at myself in the mirror. However, I managed to tolerate the chemo and get through the program and reach a milestone, my 67th birthday. The odds of my reaching this milestone had been quite bad, so I accepted the chance to celebrate with deep gratitude and thanks to the Lord.

This birthday, the third since the onset of my cancer, was the occasion for some deep spiritual reflection. (See Appendix 3 for an excerpt from his journals on his 67th birthday). I seemed to cover the full range of emotions, from deep melancholy to final uplifting "acceptance" once again. My melancholy side was saying: "You're winding down fast, this disease is now starting to win the battle." But then my positive side asserted itself. I felt grateful for the blessings I had received. God had been good to me. He gave me His peace two years ago in a lonely hospital room and it has never left me. Psalm 34 came back to me, Helen's gift, and I repeated to myself: "This poor man cried out to the Lord and He heard him and saved him out of all his troubles."

But in spite of this wonderful gift of peace, to be human is to be subject to the ups and downs of our emotions, which never give us complete rest. I was only experiencing what Jesus told us to expect. He never promised us a rose garden. He simply commanded us to "pick up your cross and follow me." Just reflecting on these primal truths brings my life back into focus and I begin to "feel better." I've reestablished my acceptance, my surrender to the will of God. This is the true road to peace.

This better part of me wants to say: "Lead on Lord. I will follow you all the way, for you alone are the way, the truth and the life." Pick me up when my faith wavers, which it surely will. Reach your hand out to me as you did to Peter when he wavered in his faith and was sinking in the turbulent sea. But behind all the assurances lies the haunting phrase from the Gospel of John which seeps into my mind, reflecting the apprehension that is always there: "taking you to places you would rather not go."

But in the long run and in the final chapter, the author of my life story will give me the goodness and love we all yearn for. That is the promise we live by and the destiny God has prepared for us. I reflected on the irony of life. Here I was, 67 years old, on the downside of my life and in many ways, I yearned to be a child again, to simply give my complete love and trust in childlike innocence to my father who will take care of me. Again, I am guilty of plagiarizing the incomparable words of the Lord who said, "Unless you become like little children, you will not enter the kingdom of heaven."

Birthdays are truly special days, the day where the unique gift of an individual can truly be celebrated. One of my favorite spiritual authors, Henri Nouwen, made the comment in his book "Here and Now," that the birthday is truly the only day we can say to our brother or sister, "I appreciate your life. I love you for being you and making my life so much richer for knowing you."

For my birthday we had a family "gathering" at Joe's house to celebrate Pop's birthday. All the people I love were there, the complete circle, and I reigned supreme as the oldest one, the patriarch, although I found myself cast in a role I was not prepared for. That evening I said something to Nancy that came out of the blue which caught her a little by surprise, perhaps me as well. I said that if I didn't have my family, all of them who were there at the "gathering," I wouldn't care so much whether I continued to live with the cancer. As I thought about that, did I really mean it? I'm really not quite sure. But I am sure about one thing. The family gives meaning to my life. The reality is there. I fathered four great children and they have given me wonderful grandchildren. A part of me is in all of them. As long as I live they will be mine to "care for," even when all I have to give is my daily prayers for each of them.

I'm not really an emotional man (to my regret) and find it difficult to express love emotionally, to "get close" to the people I love (again to my regret). But I suppose there is a great deal of truth to the maxim that you will know them by their actions. I'm sure that each member of our family knows how I feel just as I know, without reservation, how much they love me.

Because of these deepest of feelings, the person suffering a terminal illness can feel guilt over the pain being experienced by those you love. You wish you could spare them this pain and anxiety. Yet, your rational self says this is the only way – to share fully and in every way the lives of the members, where all become one.

Paul exhorts us as Christians to "put on the new man," that we are no longer who we were; we are a "new creation." I sometimes feel cheated that I was given the gift of faith so early. When I was born, I did not experience the euphoria the emotional joy that is so evident in those who receive God's amazing grace later in life. My grace came from 2000 years of ancestry, no doubt ruptured at times, but unbroken in unity and purpose, which has shaped and given meaning to so many lives. I'm an integral part of that communion of "saints" (interpreted in the broadest sense) and happy to "fit it" and belong to the people of God in my family setting. Unfortunately, we tend to take these blessings for granted and perhaps in that sense, need to be renewed and "born again."

When I think of the tortuous route Augustine took in arriving at his preeminent position as a revered father of the Church, should I wonder at my own limitations? The breakthroughs in his life came after many years of soul searching and frustration. But grace is a limitless, never-ending fountain of wisdom and knowledge, which unfolds throughout the history of mankind and can allow us to gradually enter into a life with God, into the mystery of the Trinity. The Kingdom will come.

There is no question that I am not the man I was. This "catastrophic" illness has made me a different person. Strangely enough, the physical changes, as profound as they are, are not the most significant ones. The real changes have taken place in my "inner man," that part of me that defines me and lets me know who I am and where I fit into this world.

On the down side, I have lost my vitality and my physical strength. I have become much more dependent upon others and continue to find ways of placating my ruptured ego and its needs, the very source of the energy and power which drove this machine for so many years. The negative feelings these physical changes have created must continuously be squelched and put in the proper perspective. This is an important part of the "acceptance game" and is not easy, but is the only antidote in the long run to a life of melancholy and hopelessness.

Acceptance is a nice, placid word that has a soft connotation of peace and tranquility. Yet, it can be most elusive and take much effort to acquire. At a time in our culture of burgeoning robust health in senior citizen population, a cancer patient sees himself wearing down to extinction while all those recreating seniors are now enjoying the pleasures of the young. You want that additional twenty years of the good life that is being denied you. You observe your well-tanned friends winding their way up north to see the grandchildren to share the happiness of birthdays, graduations, holidays, and weddings. You had expected to share those pleasant times. They put a nice cap on your life – a sunset of fulfillment and completion. You want to be part of the celebrations and you know you won't be for much longer and you feel cheated.

But is there an upside to all this? Between the doom and gloom and obvious depravations of this life are there glimmers of light and hope? Where is all this meaning in suffering one is expected to find?

Strangely enough it's there if you look for it and acknowledge it. It is buried deeply beneath the pain and suffering. It didn't come in big ways, but in many changes that have occurred, recreating me in a different mold, in a sense remaking me in the image of what John calls "the new man." No question about it, I am a new man in many deep and significant ways. My whole spiritual life has been turned around and I now see and experience the "big picture." From the microcosm of my former narrow provincial outlook, I have found myself moving steadily into the macrocosm of the universe at large, into that world of unity and centeredness where "all is in all."

This is the world of God, the world of the eternal, which we have always been invited to enter. But most only touch the edges, being so absorbed and distracted by the minutia of our smaller, secular lives. This metamorphosis can be at times truly profound when you allow yourself to enter fully into it. This is the world I want to enter into more and more each day as my illness progresses. I know it is the world of peace and tranquility I need as I make the transition from this life to the next.

I suspect that this transition is not easy for those who are so intimately earth bound, those who derive their knowledge and feelings from only a sensate nature. One might ask why anyone should want to surrender his individuality and autonomy into a collective consciousness where you become lost in a totality, even though you call that totality God. The truth of the matter is you would not lose your individuality. I want to preserve at all costs the personality I know as distinctively and uniquely me. I want to preserve that at all costs. And theologians say I will. They say as we move into the totality of the life through the Trinity, we become increasingly nuanced. We become more unique as individuals, rather than less, being constantly improved by the presence of God and our participation in His life. That is a beautiful, complete picture of beatitude and fulfillment, the culmination of the search that Augustine so aptly describes when he calls us "ever restless until we rest in thee".

It's not hard to discern where my hopes for peace and reconciliation to my illness lie – strictly in the providence and care of God who truly constitutes the "big picture." So long as I keep myself tethered to my former temporal life, which is waning, I will be despondent and unhappy. I will be living off negatives, dwelling in the past and without future connection. To the degree that I can learn to live in the eternal now, with my perspective anchored firmly in the big picture, the eternal world of God, I can live my life with a sense of peace and through the acceptance of true reality.

There are other more mundane components that are great gifts in my journey with cancer. I have never experienced a closer more meaningful presence of my family life. As we have traveled together through the ups and downs of almost three years of my illness, we have all grown in the love and

caring that constitutes the most basic of human relations. Each has suffered anguish and pain, each has shared in the occasional joys and good news that would break through, and above all, each has discovered a new dimension of what it means to love someone. While a good measure of love and caring has always been an integral part of our family life, I have no doubt that my illness has added substance and meaning of a special sort that would not have been there without it.

After consultation with my doctor we decided on another ten-week program of chemotherapy, even though I was apprehensive about how much of these powerful chemicals I could continue to absorb. In terms of timing, I would be finished with my treatment before the onset of the Christmas holidays. Since the options are so limited at this stage of my disease, the action we were taking seemed to be the only course that made some sense. Long shots sometimes come through.

In the week that followed I continued to feel tired and fatigued but was determined to live with it, to "grin and bear it" so to speak. It's difficult for a committed Stoic to break this mold and all my life I have had this disposition. Increased doses of morphine were alleviating much of the pain in my arm where the cancer had attacked the bone. I was thankful for that blessing.

We never seem to acquire completely that ability to turn off the teeming mind, in spite of our valiant efforts to live in the eternal now. When episodes of pain arise, and before you get it under control with additional painkillers, you experience unthwarted pain and you have a distinct sense that it can become an unbearable experience.

I found myself becoming more preoccupied with this fear of pain since I instinctively knew there would be more of it in my future. The reading material I had access to convinced me that the mind/matter connection had to play a major role in pain. Pain itself, the actual physical phenomenon of the nervous system under attack is one thing. The perception in our consciousness of what that pain is can be a quite different matter.

Research indicates rather convincingly that mind-altering techniques can work. Relaxation, hypnosis, meditation, bio-feedback and similar therapies that affect the mind and the body can work effectively for many people, but no doubt, required a lot of work to master. I hope I can achieve this. I will definitely explore this further in preparation for what might lie ahead. The one thing that I must guard against, though, is the natural tendency to become absorbed by it, to allow an inordinate fear to take control of my mind. The problem of pain will not go away. I suspect my only real alternative will be to accept it, to live with it and to have faith in a compassionate Lord not to give me more than I can bear. The latter therapy is my real "ace in the hole" and the one I will likely depend on.

CHAPTER VIII: FINAL DAYS

I find myself more and more realizing that I am slipping into my final days. Unless the good Lord decides to give me my second miracle, I'm definitely on a short-term schedule. The best medical people tell you to "listen to your body," which I do, and it is telling me rather convincingly that little by little this disease is having its way and I am reaching the end of the story.

I do not feel any great sadness. I do not feel any panic or great fear. Apprehension, melancholy, fear of the unknown, the continuous battle with doubt and uncertainty – all of these feelings are there, but underneath them all is a "quiet acceptance." I believe what peace I have received is a gift of God and is the major strength, the bedrock, on which my present mindset is based. It is the major factor that will carry me through and I thank God for it.

Whether you like to think about it or not, some very practical matters enter the picture and must be dealt with. One of the more troublesome problems arises in the area of home care. What happens when this disease reaches a point where, physically, my wife cannot take care of me at home? At what point do we make a judgment that home care is no longer practical? These are tough decisions but have to be faced. I know the time to face them is now, when at least we can look at the problem more dispassionately and not get caught up in an emotional time when urgency and a balanced approach may be at odds with one another. It may be practical for a very short-term period, but not beyond that. I know deep down I could not handle too much of this.

What about nursing homes or hospices? I have had experience with both care at home and nursing home care for my mother and father. Care at home reaches a point where it is totally time consuming, draining on the emotions and physically very demanding. A point where it becomes almost impossible. But the nursing home experience can become good or bad. Assuming the facilities are reasonably good, and in my parents' case they were good, we can then look at the level of care, which is the area that causes most of the trouble. Personnel working in nursing homes are working a tough environment. It is a very demanding and unrewarding job, leading to a quick burn out. A patient with full use of his reasoning faculties in a clean, pleasant setting can lead a reasonably good life in a nursing home, as was the case with my father. A patient who is in late stages of Alzheimer's disease, with little or no faculties remaining is a different story. It is pathetic from an emotional point of view, probably harder on the family than on the patient, who really is no longer a "person" as such.

Trying to visualize yourself in a nursing home environment is a strange experience – like who – me? It just doesn't seem to fit. But be that as it may, here I am assigned to a small room in a nice facility preparing myself mentally to get used to this little space in the universe that will be mine to inhabit for the rest of my life. It's home now.

Since reading, meditation, enjoying good music and some limited television will occupy most of my time from now on, I make certain the accommodations for these amenities are in order. Important, everything looks good, hopefully, but subject to whatever physical limitations I may have I will have exposure to fellow patients and some common area where the "community" blends together.

Hospice care is largely an unknown to me, but there are aspects of it that appeal to me. It is a by-product of the holistic movement and should provide an opportunity to spend one's last days in a "caring" environment where an aura of spirituality and human concern may pervade the facility. Since all of the patients are terminal there should be a greater sense of shared meaning and current life experience even though the degree of suffering present may have some negative effects. Considering the uncertainty of time for me, I better get busy and do some research into this area.

The holidays are over now, holidays I never expected to see and we're well into January 1995. When I realize that February 13th will be the third year since my operations, I am just amazed. So much has happened, both good and bad, you just can't imagine where this time went.

How long should we prolong life when the patient has no chance of recovery? Should extraordinary means be used? Who is best qualified to make this decision? What are the moral implications of these questions? These questions are certainly provocative from an academic point of view; from a personal point of view, when facing them for yourself, they take on a much more dramatic dimension.

While my present life continues to have meaning and I am not suffering excruciating pain, I would certainly want to continue living. When one is living a nightmare of unrelieved pain and suffering and knows the outcome is hopeless, then I would pray for a peaceful and blessed ending of my life. But what about so-called "heroic" means of survival, such as life support systems, intravenous or forced feeding and other more sophisticated techniques now available through modern technology?

I can state unequivocally and with conviction that I do not want these options used when I reach this state. I would want to make certain that my family is well aware of my conviction and would take the appropriate measures to carry it out. From my point of view, it is a family decision with my wife being the final voice. My attending doctors should also be made aware of my wishes. The need for living wills and other legal devices covering these matters is not necessary. So long as my family knows my position I am content to leave it in their hands.

Looking at the moral aspects of these decisions, I do not foresee any problem. The Church has made it abundantly clear that the so-called Death with Dignity approach where all-natural functions of the human body are not artificially repressed or altered is certainly permitted. I would not want to personally define what are meant by "heroic" means but I'm sure the medical people could clarify this for all those involved in decision-making. If a moral question still arises, I'm sure my family could get good counsel from the Church.

I'm scheduled to visit my oncologist this week and make a decision on what additional therapy, if any, I should undergo. Based upon my negative experiences with side effects this last go-round, I have made up my mind not to take any more chemotherapy. There seems little likelihood of additional therapy doing any good so why undergo the severe side effects. I doubt that Dr. Spiritos will disagree with this decision although he may want additional tests taken to ascertain to where the cancer has spread.

This brings this little narrative to a close, not because the journey I have been depicting is complete, but rather because what will happen next has not yet happened and who among us can predict the future. At this point in my life I am relatively at peace with myself, with my family and hopefully with my Lord and my God. Life has been good to me and in those moments when I can transcend my temporal nature and move closer to that "higher plane," I am certain that a better life awaits me as the promises of the Lord are accomplished and I truly enter the Father's Kingdom.

When the TV show we are watching cuts off abruptly with the tag line 'to be continued', we feel frustrated. I'm sorry to put the reader in this position but hopefully I can bring it to a close at some point in the future. As my father used to say, "God willing."

CODA

The concluding paragraph in this book was written sometime in mid-January 1995. John knew then that his remaining time was very limited. He was very sick.

In fact, his personal journal entry dated January 10 says *"I sort of hit bottom today. I walked in to the kitchen and impulsively wanted to cry. I had a hard time controlling the tears, and unfortunately Nancy was there. She came over crying, and said to me, putting her arms around me "Don't Cry." She has never seen me cry."*

We know his book was completed shortly after this January 10 date.

The ending paragraph to chapter eight might feel incomplete, perhaps contrived, too literary, maybe even abrupt. That said, we see here that an important task was completed. A faithful soldier did his job. In fact, John makes no reference in his remaining private journal entries (there were two) to completing this task. Also, he never told anyone that we know of other than perhaps his wife that he completed this task. Two months later, John died.

The excerpts from his private journals and the timelines in the appendices will help you understand more completely his faith and his courage and help you go deeper inside his "unwanted journey."

APPENDIX 1: A BIOGRAPHICAL PROFILE

John was born on September 26, 1927. His parents, John Bertman Ryan and Margaret McGrath Ryan were immigrants from Newfoundland, Canada. They came to the "States," the shorthand way they often talked, as a young married couple. He had an older sister, Peggy, and a younger brother Bob. The family grew up in Philadelphia's Kensington section. As a child, he went to Newfoundland with his parents. Unfortunately, we know little about that trip. That said, Newfoundland and codfish and "dunch" (Irish soda bread) were large presences in his life and later in his children's lives through their relationship with their grandparents. We had dinner with his parents almost every Sunday.

John attended North Catholic High School and played football and was active in the newspaper.

He attended LaSalle College, graduating in 1949 with a degree in Accounting. Over those years, he developed deep interests in Philosophy. He was President of the LaSalle Alumni Association. He went to graduate school for accounting and taught part time at LaSalle in the early part of his career.

John married Anne Cecilia Willox (Nancy) on February 4, 1950. They had four children, Joe, Jack, Mike, and Pat. Both our parents loved their children, their three daughters-in-law (Mary Ann, Michelle, Bernie), and their grandchildren deeply and attended all their big events. They had eight grandchildren: Kevin, Kate, Kelly, Colleen, Michael (Motts), Matt, John, Jonathan. His last grandchild, Jonathan, was born after he passed. Pat's husband, Bob Dice, never knew John or Nancy but he is "pure Ryan" to the core.

Summer vacations at the Jersey Shore were a family ritual and we all have wonderful memories of family picnics, both as children and as adults.

In later years, as adults with children ourselves, we all remember "the little picnics" at Weymouth Place, their home.

John worked for Horn and Hardart (H&H) in Philadelphia, a pioneer in the food automat business, and rose through ranks. He became an officer of this iconic company in his 40s. After H&H, he ran a large region, the North East region, for Macke, a vending company.

At the end of his career, with his brother Bob, he launched and ran a small private seafood restaurant and take out business.

He was an accomplished executive. He knew the ups and downs of business. He knew hard times. He was a quiet leader, "steady" is a better word.

He was a Roman Catholic. He attended Mass faithfully his entire life. His faith deepened during his illness. John was a family man. He was always there for birthdays and other special moments. He mentored all four of his children.

APPENDIX 2:
CHRONOLOGY OF JOHN'S ILLNESS

This chronology was reconstructed from John's private journal. We never asked for his medical records. As such, we cannot document the particulars concerning his surgery, how much of his stomach and esophagus were removed, where the cancer advanced to, the meds he took, and so on. That said, John felt he received very good medical care. He developed an excellent working relationship with several of the MDs and wrote about them in his journal.

<u>1992</u>

February 13: Operation at Holy Redeemer Hospital in Abington, PA. The operation confirmed he had advanced stomach cancer.

March 26: He got a second opinion concerning treatment options with a specialist at the Hospital of the University of Pennsylvania.

April 15: He started chemotherapy. Five days of treatment and then three weeks to recover from the effects.

May 22: He completed a second series of chemo treatments.

July 24: He began five weeks of radiation.

August 2: He began another 10 weeks of chemotherapy.

October 24: All tests were "just fine;" no evidence of cancer.

1993

A year of remission. We have no good record of his medical visits and condition during this time period. In fact, he only wrote two journal entries that year.

1994

January 13: In his journal, John noted there is "a 50/50 chance" of the cancer returning.

February 13: This was his second year free of cancer; he wrote letters of gratitude.

April 16: A setback; the cancer returns.

May 6: In his journal, John writes he believes he has 5-6 months to live, at best a year.

May 14: He completed the first week of radiation.

June 11: His weight is at 138.

November 28: He is experiencing great fatigue. The system is winding down, he wrote; his weight is at its lowest point – 128 (later in 1995, it goes to 118).

December 1: In his journal, John said it was an "amazingly good day" as he worked on his book.

1995

January 10: In his journal, he wrote that he "hit bottom" and he cried in private. He was at home and cared for by his wife. He received meds for pain control. He received no formal nursing care or hospice care.

January 24: The last journal entry.

March 23: I took my father to Holy Redeemer hospital because of the large swelling in his legs, ankles, and feet. He also had pain in his left arm, left shoulder, and back, where the cancer had traveled. He was in the hospital for 6 days.

March 29: 7:30 PM he died at the hospital.

APPENDIX 3: HIS PRIVATE JOURNAL

We excerpt below four entries from John's private journal. That journal was longer than the book (31,080 words; 91 entries in total). Nine entries written in 1992, two written in 1993, and 56 written in 1994, the year he often prayed for a second miracle.

We have honored his intention here that this be a private and confidential document. It is raw in the best sense and unedited. It reveals an honest inquiry and effort at sense making.

The excerpts were chosen using the following logic:

- His first entry

- His last two entries

- His longest entry

These four entries give us a sense of his realism; his anguish at times; what counted as a good day; his love for his family; his hopes; his belief in "the eternal now."

First Journal Entry, March 1992 (no specific date)

My reflections and feelings as I progress on this unwanted journey. Cancer is not a good companion. I would rather choose another. But, cancer is the one I have been given and I will do my best to get along with him.

While I truly appreciate my loved ones, who unselfishly reach out to me and want to accompany me on this journey, it is cancer himself who defines our relationship and sets the course, leading me "to places I would rather not go." He does not welcome company on the way. He wants to possess and dominate me every waking hour.

I break away from him at every opportunity, but very shortly he reasserts his authority and dominates my life once again. Many great thinkers say there is "meaning" in everything, even sickness and death. Perhaps I will find the meaning of my cancer. I will certainly try.

As this journey progresses to its appointed end, I hope and pray that God will not give me more than I can bear. Way down deep, I trust that he will take care of me.

Last Two Entries

January 19, 1995

Visit with Dr. Spiritos. Michael went with us. Nice visit. We covered the waterfront. He does not want any more chemo. Feels it is doing no good. I agree. This can always be considered later, but I feel he will continue to oppose it.

Morphine – we had extensive conversation on its use and efficacy. Apparently, there is no "upper limit" to use of this drug. He has used dosages in the thousands. So, my current intake is really on the lower side. I can use the time release and supplement it with the fast-acting type.

New program – 90 MG in AM. 90 MG going to bed and 60 MG in between. He also recommended taking 2 Motrin with PM dose. This apparently helps control bone pain. There is nothing to stop me from taking as much morphine as I need; no point to "save it" for later use (not as long as he can keep going up on dosage). This is reassuring insofar as I can feel confident that they will be able to control future heavy pain. I've been getting apprehensive about pain in last week. This makes me feel better.

Weight terrible. 119.5. I must get more food into me. Blood pressure 100/69. My therapy: Use pain killers to control pain, including breakthroughs as needed. Stay comfortable. Grin and bear it.

Tuesday, January 24

The weekend was pretty good physically. I seemed to have less arm pain, slept well and my appetite was even a little better. Today and yesterday I feel OK but I'm in somewhat of a "down" mood. No particular reason. Even my reading is half-hearted. I think the routine, the "sameness" day in and day out may get to me. Then again, I may be slipping away from my "higher plane." I think more time directed to prayer and meditation is in order. It seems when I get deeply into this mode I am more at peace and able to cope with my life better.

Drove downtown Saturday with Joe to visit Bishop Newman's shrine at St. Peters. Enjoyed the trip. No problems. Jack and family visited on Sunday, also Patrick, so this week we saw them all which was nice.

September 26, 1994: Longest Entry
(1600+ words – selected excerpts below were edited)

Today is my 67th birthday; it is the 3rd birthday I've "celebrated" since I contracted cancer. How do I feel? It is a good question. If you asked me that question this morning, I would have said unequivocally and with candor, I feel thankful and grateful. I didn't expect to be here for my 2nd birthday after cancer arrived, but here I am for my 3rd birthday A.C. (after cancer). That plays on symbols – B.C. and A.C. – has a lot more poignancy and meaning than one might surmise.

But ask that question now – 11:00 o'clock at night with the day of birth ready to pass into the relentless stream of other birthdays – and my answer becomes less clear, a little more melancholic and a lot more ambiguous. Why the difference? I really don't know. Perhaps my actual physical condition hit me. I pushed a fertilizer spreader around the lawn a little vigorously and sort of collapsed in a chair, panting for breadth after three or four minutes. Same with the next attempt. But, finally after four or five attempts I completed the job. That sort of finished me for the day physically. I slept several hours late in the afternoon.

The haunting thought kept recurring: you're winding down fast; this disease is starting to win the battle. Fatigue doesn't exactly inspire confidence and optimism. But why the big letdown? I've known and expected this kind of pattern all along.

I guess the same old story. Hope springs eternal, and a few days of "feeling good" lulls one into a false sense of wellbeing and physical normalcy, which just doesn't exist. Human nature thrives on delusion.

But deeper reflection on this birthday does have some special significance for me. I am grateful and I thank God from the heart that He has been good to me. He gave me His Peace in a lonely hospital room 2 1/2 years ago and he has never taken it away from me (Psalm 34: "This poor man called out to the Lord and he heard him, and saved him out of all his troubles"). But in spite of this wonderful gift, to be human is to be subject to the ups and downs of our emotions. Our consciousness, the "teeming mind" of man, which never lets one find complete rest. I am only experiencing what Jesus conditioned us to expect. He never promised us a "Rose Garden." He simply asked us to pick up our cross and follow him.

Just reflecting on these primal truths brings my life back into focus. I begin to "feel better." I've re-established my Acceptance, my Surrender to the will of God. The better part of me wants to say: "Lead on Lord." I'm following You all the way, for You alone are "the Way, the Truth, and the Life." Pick me up when I waver. Reach out your hand to me as you did to Peter when he wavered in his faith and was sinking into the rising sea. But the haunting passage from John also enters my mind "taking me to places I would rather not go." But, in the long run, I am sure that in the final chapter, the author of my life story will take care of me and bring the goodness and love which we all yearn for to me in fill measure. That is the promise we live for. That is the destiny that God has prepared for us. Funny, I'm 67 years old today – on the "old side." But in some ways, I yearn to be a child again, to simply in childlike innocence give my completed love and trust to my Father who will take care of me.

Aside from the "ups and downs" of my reflections on this birthday, I have much to be thankful for. We had another "gathering" of the family yesterday at Joe's house to celebrate "Pop's birthday."

All the people I love were there, except Jack. But I had seen him on the way to Joe's, so the circle was complete. I was the oldest there, the Patriarch, but I really didn't feel that way. Funny how time projects you into a role you're not prepared for.

I said something to Nancy the other day, which sort of came out of the blue and caught her a little bit by surprise, maybe me too. I said that if I didn't have my "family" – all of them who were at the "gathering" I wouldn't care one way or another whether I continued to live with this cancer. Even now as I think about it, did I really mean that? I'm not quite sure.

But I am sure about one thing. The family gives meaning to my life. The reality is there. I fathered four children and have wonderful grandchildren. A part of me is in all of them. So long as I live they are mine to "care for" in all ways I am capable of, even when all I have to give is my daily prayers for each of them.

I'm really not an emotional man (to my regret) and find it difficult to "love" emotionally. Difficult to "get close" to the people I love (again to my regret). But I think I would give my life for each of these people in my life, as well as my wife who shares this progeny with me.

Do I feel loved by this family of mine? Yes, I do. Without reservation. Each of my "children" loves me in their own "unique" way.

Patrick is emotional and surprisingly deep. She loves hard and continuously. She cares "deeply" and brings a special gift to the one she loves (me). People who love this hard can suffer for it. This concerns me, since I want to shield her from pain. I would rather suffer the pain myself. A daughter like Pat is a precious commodity indeed.

Joe, my oldest son, and sometimes the most enigmatic of them all. My "condition" hurts him to the quick. I saw that again yesterday when he tried to propose a light toast to my birthday and broke down emotionally. I wish with all my heart I could save him from all this "pain" and sorrow.

He is such a complex, wonderful and talented man. As a father I see qualities in him I wish I had myself, but I see a restlessness that is always there. If only he could find that peaceful place where he is able to relax, enjoy his life and find more balance in his activities. He is driven in his ambition. It worries me.

Michael is Michael. Caught up in his own world. Ambitious, super active, and always reaching for more. Thank God for the stability of Bernie and a strong family orientation. I don't really know Michael. He doesn't let you in. I know he loves me and has deep feelings about my situation but he can't confront it with me. Maybe it's just as well. I know his feelings and I'm sure he realizes that.

And that brings me to Jack, in some ways the best of all. I love Jack for his human qualities. He is so simple and so vulnerable. He has always been that way. I still have the vivid image of him as a skinny little boy thrashing wildly in the water trying to win the race at the swimming pool and damn near drowning. He came in last, but not for lack of effort and heart.

Jack has had many ups and downs but he has come a long way. I am close to Jack. He has let me come inside and share some of his most intimate thoughts. Emotionally he is open and responsive. A hug to Jack is spontaneous and meaningful. To me, in spite of my aloofness, it feels good to be hugged.

Nancy felt some pain with this birthday. She knows where we are. She lives with it night and day. She has been a wonderful helpmate and caring "mother" to me. I hope I can do all in my place to ease the burden on her. But I can't always overcome my egotistical, selfish ways. I will try hard. She deserves only the best from me.

APPENDIX 4: LETTERS OF GRATITUDE

During his time of remission, John wrote six letters of gratitude, one to each of his four children and one each to his sister and brother. He did not to write a letter to his wife. He reflected in his journal on that decision saying Nancy "knew all" this. He said, "words were not needed," yet at the same time, you sense he was unsure in looking back and thinking more about it. These letters were two pages long, heartfelt, deeply inspiring. There were no wasted words. They communicated substantive messages. They are literally priceless. See below a copy of his handwritten February 13, 1994 letter to his daughter.

Dear Patrick,

It is very unusual for me to write a letter. However, today marks a very special occasion for me and I want to express some thoughts, which may be best expressed in the form of a letter.

Two years ago on this date I was operated on for cancer. My future at that time seemed quite bleak and, frankly, I did not expect to last six months. Now, two years later I am still here and doing very well.

A healing? Without question. A cure? Quite possible. Neither could have happened without a combination of factors, which came together to see me through. The healing power of prayer and the tremendous support of family and friends were at the top of the list. Patrick (Pat), I want you to know how important your love and support were to me during that very traumatic time in my life. You were there in body, heart and spirit to help me when I needed help, and you are still there today.

Neither you nor I will ever forget those first days when the doctor informed us of the Big C. There is no other shock quite like it and I know in those moments what you were feeling. I wish I could have spared you that anguish. But, I was so glad you were there because there is something very special about the tender relationship between father and daughter. Also, some things just can't be borne alone.

Patrick, this letter was not intended to wallow in undue maudlin sentimentality, as real as it is, so I will cut if off now. A feel a sense of JOY! They say that out of adversity comes strength. I cannot predict nor control the future, but as a result of this unwanted experience, I have been raised to a new level of faith and trust and no longer have the same degree of fear and anxiety that is so much a part of the human condition. Let's simply say I have a quiet confidence that regardless of what the future holds for me, I will be given the strength to handle it. After all, the master psychologist and healer told us: "Fear is useless, what is needed is TRUST."

Perhaps we can all learn from adversity and take life as it comes. We must enjoy the good things when they come and weather the storm when the bad things come along ...... and always be thankful for what we do have, particularly for those who love us.

Thanks again, Patrick, for being there. I wanted to share these few thoughts with you on this day of thanks and thanksgiving for me. You know I will always be there for you.

With love,
JPR

P.S. I can't tell you how important it was to me when you were there to support and comfort your mother when she needed you most. As a result, she was a tower of 'unsuspected' strength.

APPENDIX 5: LETTER TO A MEN'S FAITH SHARING GROUP

John was asked to talk at a meeting of the Men's Faith Sharing Group at his Church. Below are excerpts from a long letter, 5 pages, typed, not hand written like his journals and the draft of his book. We do not know who typed this letter. He did not have a typewriter or computer in his house. He wrote this letter on September 7, 1994. We see John as an excellent teacher. A fellow traveler facing the hard questions, importantly, sharing his lessons learned.

Dear Bob:

I write this letter with regrets that I cannot attend the meeting of the Men's Faith Sharing Group on Saturday morning.

I have had a recurrence of my cancer and am in the middle of my radiation/chemotherapy regimen. This leaves one totally fatigued at certain points and restricted in your activities.

I only attended one of your meetings, at St. Bede's, my home parish, and was greatly impressed and spiritually nourished by the faith of "The Brothers of Christ" who were present. I truly felt like one of you.

I had an opportunity to share my cancer experience with a small group of your members led by Dom Lettieri. This was a new experience for me, since by nature I tend to be introspective and private, particularly in my spiritual life, yet the example of others brings one out of his shell.

I repeat that experience here, since it is a necessary backdrop to understand my reflections on Mathew 5 and 6, which unfortunately I cannot discuss at the meeting. (He then provides a

3-page factual summary of his journey with cancer).

And finally, some reflections on Mathew 5 and 6, which in some ways will probably be a "retrospective" on my own spiritual life.

The sermon on the mount raises many provocative and troubling personal questions:

-Have I followed the sermon on the mount in my own personal life?

-Did I hunger and thirst after justice, actively pursuing it, or did I give it lip service?

-Was I a peacemaker?

-Did I suffer for my principles and my faith and take the ridicule of the crowd, or did I wimp out and fail to step forward with faith and courage?

Looking back, I think my heart was in the right direction since I never knowingly and with malice tried to hurt someone. My failures were more failures of omission – opportunities lost – the many good things I could have done that I didn't do.

Being the "Light of the World," I allowed my light to grow dim. I did not let it "shine forth" as I should have done.

Did I truly forgive my brother and seek his pardon? Yes, I think I learned early in life that hatred and enmity in one's heart destroys you. You cannot live with yourself.

Did I turn the other cheek? Sometimes. This is a hard dictum to follow. Our pride gets in the way.

I was not ostentatious in my prayer life… if anything, I was too private, too much of the spectator living in spiritual isolation. While it is wrong to flaunt one's piety and prayer life, it is equally wrong to isolate yourself from the communal worship of God.

One of the more meaningful passages I thought about is the one on false values, storing up this world's treasure at the expense of spiritual values. It is so true "for where your treasure is, there will your heart be also."

This passage reminds me of the ancient Greek aphorism, Socrates I believe: "A man becomes what he loves." We see this in the saints, who became what they loved… life of Francis of Assisi, who became almost a second Christ. I think now I didn't live enough to become what I want to be. It takes a lifetime to know this truth. But having hope we must stay on the right path.

The simplicity and the beauty of the Lord's prayer is obscured by its familiarity. We are too close to fully appreciate its message. It defines in the clearest terms the basic relationship between a loving father and his created children; it is an immutable paradigm for life.

Trust in providence… those of us who have faced serious illness and learned to live with it know full well what trust in providence can do. It can move mountains. It teaches us that "fear is useless and what is needed is trust (love)" for after all else, love is the moving force of life. It leads to God and partakes of God since God Is Love – the source of all other love and its perfect manifestation and presence.

The final passage in Chapter 6 is a thing of beauty: "Set your heart on the Kingdom of God… and all these other things will be given to you as well. So, do not worry about tomorrow; tomorrow will take care of itself; Each day has trouble enough of its own."

Great, great advice! Wonderful to cultivate when things go right. Life saving when things go wrong.

The serenity prayer and the popular aphorism of "One day at a time" could have been scripted directly out of this passage.

Enough reflections for now on this rich source of wisdom. I would have liked to share these thoughts with the others and benefitted from their insights. It is my loss.

My apologies for the long narrative on my illness and its effect on my life. I didn't intend to ramble on but it may be a story that can be shared by a kindred soul who faces this dilemma. There is both comfort and faith in shared misery. God's grace is ubiquitous in this world. We will find it if we ask for it.

With Trust and Hope,
John P. Ryan

APPENDIX 6: NANCY'S NOTES

By early November of 1995, John's book had been typed and read by the whole family. John's wife, Nancy, wanted to share her observations and feelings, so she wrote notes for a meeting with her family on a Saturday morning at her Weymouth Place home.

They were typed up and addressed to Bruce White, a friend of the family, who had been a journalist.

Nancy's notes below give you a window into her world. Her notes are honest, heartfelt, clear, simple, not convoluted, not self-focused, not self-absorbed, full of realism and caring. She grieved but was not filled with regret or bitterness. She too traveled this hard path with her husband. She too changed. Her own character strengths deepened and flourished. We all saw that. She made do, was resourceful, had grit, remained a masterful friend to many. I think she became her true self in the end.

Dear Bruce,

Here are my notes. If you have any problems, please call. Again, many thanks for your help. Hope you and your family have a nice Thanksgiving.

- I, his wife, was scared. I was afraid. It was cancer but I didn't want to admit it. What would I do without him? I was so dependent on him.

- I was angry. I was not prepared to hear his cold blunt remarks (the oncologist).

- Every night, the last thing we would do before bed was say the Rosary in thanksgiving for a good day, for the ability to eat that day, and all the intentions that we prayed for. It was a wonderful and peaceful experience.

- Oh, what a day! We cried. We hugged. We praised God for his goodness. We held each other. We danced around the kitchen. We were like two little kids. It was great.

- I had a dream. I was crying and feeling sorry for myself, and wanting everyone to know my husband was a victim of cancer and wanted the company I was with to stop their small talk. I was awakened by the presence of Jack's arm around my shoulder telling me, "it's all right." I know he is still taking care of me.

- Things were not the same. He was not the man he was six months ago but he did his best to fool us all.

- Bedtime was hard on him. He needed help to get undressed, take medicine, and try to get as warm and comfortable as possible. He was lucky if he got four hours sleep and then more medicine.

- This was it. What I so dreaded. The Doctor said 3-6 months. How do I tell the rest of my family? Reality is here. God please help me. He did.

- We all know he is getting weaker. Everybody is doing their part to spend as much time with him as possible. He has fulfilled a lot of his desires. He has been able to show his emotions. He has hugged everyone, saying it was necessary to touch and be held. We spoke about death, final arrangements, and both understood what each wanted when our final time would come. He said he was not afraid.

- Final remark: no one can write their final chapter of life but all of my husband's dreams and wishes were fulfilled. He passed away on March 29th with complications from cancer and pneumonia. He went to "His Maker" with peace and dignity surrounded by all of his loved ones. He taught us a lot. The meaning of love. Not to be afraid but to trust. I am grateful that I was given the strength and courage to care for him. I know he was able to say "Thy will be done."

APPENDIX 7: SEAFOOD AMERICA

John and his younger brother, Bob, invested in and started a seafood restaurant and takeout business in 1985. This family business venture proved to be unsuccessful, even with all the hard work and long hours. There were serious cash problems in the last years of the business.

The business was sold after John got sick but it really needed to be sold years earlier. John wrote about that painful work experience in his book. He wondered how and in what ways that stress accelerated the growth of his cancer cells. He knew there was a connection. That said, few things in life are black and white. There are large gray zones. There are large and small dilemmas in all lives. His son Jack worked with him in this venture. They lived through those problems. They learned much from each other as they moved forward. They learned to endure and to make sense of difficulties. We see below "good moments," important rituals, found during that difficult time. The notes below were written by his son, Jack, in November 1995, just about six months after his father passed.

"I had the privilege and, at times, the headaches of working in the family restaurant. I helped build the unit. Also, I helped sell the unit and that was not easy. There are a couple of stories that I enjoy thinking about. One time when the business was doing OK, just paying the bills and my salary, there was a newspaper reporter who came in for lunch. We started talking and the next week this man wrote a great article about how much he enjoyed the restaurant.

However, the one thing that stands out in my mind the most is that Dad built the business up, but he gave me the credit for the restaurant doing so well.

Dad never promoted himself. He was a very intelligent, well-rounded, and gentle man.

One final story shows a nice lesson that he taught me and his employees. Toward the end of the business, right before Dad got sick, he worked the kitchen, the "back of the house," he called it. He cooked and cleaned to save labor when we needed to cut hours. But every day, he took a break to watch the sunset. He urged all the employees to do the same. So that became a ritual. Every night when it was possible, all the employees who were in the kitchen took a couple of minutes to watch the sun set. The lesson from this is clear. Don't get too wrapped up in work--enjoy the beautiful nature that is all around us. Eventually, all the employees looked forward to watching the sunset with Mr. Ryan".

AFTERWORD

Remembering, Then and Now

The notes below were written a few days after my Dad passed. His family stood guard. I remember his last gesture, reaching out, no words spoken, his eyes were the bridge we walked on. Then, he left us. As time goes by, the images and the memories become more remote but the meaning of his life, his journey with cancer, his courage, his unfathomable love for his family, becomes clearer. In his absence, he is present more.

He was Never Alone: In Memoriam

Thursday, March 23, 1995. I took my father to the hospital because of the large swelling in his legs, ankles, and feet. He knew in the way you don't know that you know, as we sat in the Friendly's restaurant waiting for his admission paperwork to be completed. I did not realize how close to the end it was. He died six days later.

I knew from the beginning that my father was dying, that his cancer was terminal. Over a three-year period, the stomach cancer had traveled through the continents of his strong body to his now frail legs, left arm, left shoulder, back, and to other unknown regions. He knew pain. He never camouflaged his cancer and I never denied the seriousness and finality of his illness. What I remember about my father is archetypal, constant, like the changing of the seasons, not a specific moment or one special conversation. I remember him living, living in all his dying.

Sunday, March 26, 1995. There was no big conversation or words of consolation this day. He was fully conscious. Much himself–organized, wanting complete medical information, adapting without anger to the rituals of hospital life and the rhythms of the day.

The important conversations and messages had long ago been spoken. All through his illness, he talked honestly and openly and directly about death, the eternal now, his transition period, his children, his wife, himself–his regrets, misfortunes, accomplishments, preparing for this final journey. And I knew without question the depth of my father's feelings for me. He gave me his journals at the end. He entered a place where there was no need for journals, or for reading, for complicated conversations, for big words. That part of himself he gave away – to my brothers and sister, my mother, others.

What I remember about that last beautiful day are small things. Eating home-made rhubarb with him for breakfast. His clear, strong voice in making the decision not to take the barium treatment and doing this without consulting any of his family. His deep courage, a physical courage like the warrior. His inner strength, gentle strengths.

I remember shaving my dad in the early afternoon before visitors came. It was a private time. He had a thick beard. I remember feeling close to him. I remember warmth, quiet, the hospital room, touching his face. Conversation and words were not part of this day.

I remember my mother "dressing up" to see my father in the hospital. She drove their car that day with Patty. I saw my mother wanting to be pleasing to him, showing her love for him. I remember their small talk. I remember Mom's new shoes. I remember Dad's thick-soled black shoes. They were Italian. He wore those shoes that Thursday to the hospital. (Later I learned that my brother Michael's family gave him those shoes as a Christmas gift and that made me happy.) I remember Patty and the afternoon hours, sunlight. I remember his swollen legs and feet. I remember his enormous exhaustion that night. I remember his sitting on the edge of the bed gasping for breath. I remember lifting him up and the fragility of his body. I remember his sipping ginger ale and his lips puckering with the tartness.

I remember leaving. Not being afraid. Not understanding fully. And returning late Monday night when he was no longer conscious. I remember that he remembered, for a brief moment, that Patty, Kevin, Mary Ann and I returned from our trip and we were there. Time stopped for one day in our need to return home. Children again. And then he slowly went away. And I remember thinking he was pure, like a mummy wrapped in white sheets ready for his final journey. And I remember being very proud of him.

My father died on Wednesday, March 29, at 7:30 pm. He took his last breath in private. We were all nearby. I remember my mother being sensitive to his privacy. His family, all his grandchildren, his sister and brother, his close friends, Harry and Joan, were with him during his last two days and nights of his life. He was never alone.

ACKNOWLEDGEMENTS

This book has long been in the making. It began as a Saturday morning conversation in October of 1996 with my Mother, my two brothers, my sister, and a friend, Bruce White. Wise words from an Italian song, however, tell the deeper story and significance of this project. Nine simple words: "The years teach much that the days never knew". Much truth here. We are grateful above all to my Dad for leaving us his handwritten book manuscript and his journals and, importantly, for what we have learned from him, then and now.

Many individuals generously gave of their time and provided counsel to advance this book. These fellow travelers include Pat Ryan Dice, Bruce White, Larry Churchill, the late Renee Fox, Jack Ryan, Mike Ryan, Kelly Ryan, Kevin Ryan, and Mary Ann Ryan. All played large roles in shaping this final book. Many others read this book and helped this book find the light of day. Thankful for the late John Costa, Arthur Kleinman MD, Nan Dobson, Karen Wall, Ted Gambill, Eileen Pitone, Bob Waldron, Pat Keegan MD, Bob Fisher, Mary Lou Quinlan, Deanna Thompson, Richard Quinney, Mickey Braswell, Morhaf Al Achkar MD, Jim McDowell, Phil Friedrich, Stephen Murray, Asya Blue. Special thanks to Alana Ryan for our cover photo. This sunrise photo was taken on the beach in Avalon, NJ. That beach was a place special to my Dad and remains a very special place to my family.

For further information and resources: see the web site – **JohnPRyanSr.com**.

Made in the USA
Monee, IL
19 March 2021